# The
# FARMHOUSE KITCHEN
# COOKBOOK

# The
# FARMHOUSE KITCHEN
# COOKBOOK

First published by Tigerprint for
Marks & Spencer.

This edition published in 1996 by Chancellor Press
an imprint of Reed International Books Ltd.,
Michelin House, 81 Fulham Road, London SW3 6RB
and Auckland, Melbourne, Singapore and Toronto

Recipes Copyright © Reed International Books Limited
Concept and Design © Reed International Books Limited

ISBN 1 85152 933 0

Produced by Mandarin Offset
Printed in Hong Kong

# CONTENTS

# INTRODUCTION

Two aims are at the heart of this collection of recipes: to make the best use of the natural ingredients found in the countryside and to carry on the traditions of the country kitchen both in terms of the type of dishes prepared and of the relaxed family atmosphere that is created when everyone assembles to enjoy the results of the cook's labours. This style of eating was based on the need to provide nourishing, wholesome food for the healthy appetites which working in the fresh air engendered.

That need has not changed throughout the years, though the fixtures and fittings of the country kitchen have greatly improved to take much of the hard work out of the preparation and the cooking of the food. We no longer cook over open fires, nor are most of us using solid fuel for heating the cooker, although kitchen ranges still have their champions and come into their own for casseroles and other slow-cooked dishes. The refrigerator and the freezer have taken the place of the larder providing a more reliable means of storing food. Several of the dishes in this collection can be made hours in advance, then stored as directed in the recipes. Others can be prepared at your own convenience and frozen for another day. Liquidizers and food processors have taken the tedium out of many of the preparation chores, releasing valuable time for the cook, and making experiment an enjoyable pastime.

## NATURAL INGREDIENTS

Start with fresh ingredients and you have a head start in providing nutritious meals. All vegetables are high in vitamins but unfortunately these are diminished by the processes of preparation and cooking. You can reduce this loss by doing the washing and slicing or chopping of the vegetables as near to the cooking time as possible and cooking them as close to the serving time as is practical. Cook the vegetables for a short time only and in a small amount of water. Serving them raw in salads is obviously the best way to conserve the vitamins, so try out the recipes for both summer and winter salads in 'The Vegetable Garden'.

Choosing home-produced vegetables in their appropriate season not only ensures fresh products but also automatically introduces variety into the dishes you prepare throughout the year. Recipes are given for both the autumn and winter vegetables – cabbage, chicory, leeks, parsnips and Jerusalem artichokes – and for the shorter season of summer vegetables, such as asparagus, broccoli, courgettes, peppers and tomatoes.

Fresh herbs enhance both vegetable and meat dishes. Suggestions for their use are given throughout the recipes but substitutions can, of course, be made and by experiment, you will find the ones best suited to you and your family's taste. A small herb garden or herbs grown in pots on the windowsill provide a choice of herbs at your fingertips. Of the herbs mentioned in this book, basil, chervil, dill and parsley are annuals, thus they need to be grown from seed or seedling each season. The remainder (chives, marjoram, mint, sage, sorrel, tarragon, thyme, rosemary) are perennials, which should come up every year, though they may die back in winter.

Herbs can be frozen either in sprigs or chopped, and will keep well for up to six months. To freeze as sprigs, simply wash them and shake dry, then pack in small freezer bags. When ready to use, the leaves can easily be stripped off the sprigs while still frozen. Alternatively, you can strip off the leaves and chop up before freezing.

As with vegetables, all fruit is high in vitamin C and blackcurrants particularly so. Their vitamins are quickly lost through contact with light, air and heat, so the advice on preparing and cooking is the same as for vegetables. The best way to eat them is as fresh as possible. With imports most fruit is available all year round but at a price. It is more economical to use fruit in season. Apples and pears are available most of the year, although not in the height of summer, when there is a marvellous variety of soft fruit, such as black and redcurrants, berries and cherries, plums, greengages and damsons. Rhubarb appears in the spring and blackberries ripen at the end of summer, just as apples are coming into season again. 'The Fruit Garden' contains an exciting range of recipes using these fruits.

Wholesome, as well as fresh, ingredients are a feature of this collection. Wholewheat flour is particularly recommended in the vegetable cobbler (page 19), the blackcurrant sesame crumble (page 92) and in several of the baking recipes in 'Country

6

Teas'. Wholewheat pasta is used in the dishes in 'Harvest Suppers'. Wholewheat flour is milled from 100% wholewheat grain and therefore includes both the wheatgerm and bran: the former contains vital vitamins and minerals, the latter the fibre essential for health and well-being. The flour should be sieved before use to break down any lumps but be sure to tip back the bran left in the sieve. Wholemeal flour is produced from 80-90% wholewheat grain and is consequently lighter than wholewheat flour.

## THE RECIPES

The chapters – four of which contain recipes based on the type of ingredient ('The Vegetable Garden', 'River, Sea and Moor', 'Farmhouse Fare' and 'The Fruit Garden') while the remaining two ('Harvest Suppers' and 'Country Teas') are concerned with the type of meal – contain a wide range of recipes from soups and salads to casseroles and roasts, from creams and ices to scones and cakes. Menu planning will depend on the requirements of your family, but should always achieve a balance between light and heavy meals, instant foods and complicated dishes.

For brunches try the omelette (page 71), the oatmeal herrings (page 36), the Arbroath smokies (page 37) or the Priddy oggies (page 74) and follow up with the fruit compote (page 88).

The salads and grilled or baked fish dishes make a delicious light lunch, especially appropriate if a country tea is planned for later in the day.

Casseroles come into their own if you are having to feed a family, which doesn't all appear for meals at the same time, whereas the game pie on page 38, the roasts and stuffed joints are ideal for those weekend meals, when the food is served and eaten at a relaxed pace.

Light desserts, such as a fruit jelly (page 88 or 90), a peach granita or the marinated nectarines (page 103) are perfect to follow these meaty meals or to complement one of the filling pasta dishes (pages 66-69).

The country kitchen is a good place to spend time in. It has all the freshest produce of the fields and farms, markets and gardens; it has warmth and it is the heart of the house, the natural attraction for all the family.

# CHAPTER ONE

# THE VEGETABLE GARDEN

Each season brings a fresh crop of succulent vegetables to serve hot or cold. In the summer, freshly-gathered garden or market produce can be chopped up and mixed in refreshing combinations for a cool lunch or picnic. For winter days there are hot accompaniments to the roast or substantial baked dishes for a satisfying family supper, as well as some crunchy salads to add variety to the normal winter fare.

# ASPARAGUS MOUSSE SALAD

*Serves 4 as a main salad or 6 as a starter*

450 g (1 lb) fresh asparagus
300 ml (½ pint) water
25 g (1 oz) butter or margarine
25 g (1 oz) plain flour
15 g (½ oz) powdered gelatine, dissolved in
2 tablespoons hot water
150 ml (¼ pint) soured cream or
plain unsweetened yogurt
grated rind of ½ lemon
1 tablespoon lemon juice
1 hard-boiled egg, shelled and finely chopped
salt
freshly ground black pepper
1 lettuce, to serve (optional)

*Preparation time: 15 minutes, plus setting*
*Cooking time: 25-40 minutes*

If fresh asparagus is not available, substitute 450 g (1 lb) frozen asparagus. Simmer the tips for 5 minutes, and the stems for 6-8 minutes, then use according to the recipe instructions.

1. Wash the asparagus and trim off any tough woody parts at the bottom of the stalks. Cut off the tips with about 5 cm (2 inches) of stem and simmer in the salted water for about 5-10 minutes until tender but not limp. Remove the tips with a slotted spoon and leave to cool.
2. Chop the remaining parts of the asparagus stems into small pieces and add to the simmering water. Cover and simmer for 15-30 minutes until soft. Drain, reserving the cooking water.
3. Make up the cooking water to 300 ml (½ pint) with water or milk. Melt the butter or margarine in a pan and stir in the flour. When smooth, gradually stir in the cooking liquid and bring to the boil, stirring until thickened. Add the drained chopped asparagus stems and simmer for 3 minutes, stirring from time to time.
4. Pour the sauce into a mixing bowl. Stir in the dissolved gelatine and leave until cool but not set.
5. Stir in the soured cream or yogurt, lemon rind and juice and chopped hard-boiled egg. Add salt and pepper to taste. Pour into a dish and chill until set.
6. To serve, arrange the lettuce leaves on individual plates. Place spoonfuls of mousse on top of the lettuce and garnish with the reserved tips.

# SPRING GREEN TERRINE

*Serves 4 as a main salad or 8 as a starter*

225 g (8 oz) streaky bacon, rinded
50 g (2 oz) butter or margarine
1 onion, peeled and chopped
1 garlic clove, peeled and crushed
350 g (12 oz) spring greens, coarse stalks removed
150 ml (¼ pint) water
salt
75 g (3 oz) breadcrumbs
2 eggs, beaten
grated nutmeg
freshly ground black pepper
2 hard-boiled eggs, shelled
salad ingredients (e.g. endive, tomato), to garnish

*Preparation time: 30 minutes*
*Cooking time: 40 minutes*
*Oven: 180°C, 350°F, Gas Mark 4*

1. Stretch the bacon rashers with the blade of a blunt knife and lay them crosswise, overlapping, in a 450 g (1 lb) loaf tin, so that top and long sides are completely covered and at least 2.5 cm (1 inch) overlaps the sides of the tin.
2. Melt the butter or margarine in a large saucepan and fry the onion for 5 minutes, then add the garlic.
3. Wash the spring green leaves and shred them finely. Add to the pan with the water and some salt. Cover and cook for 10-15 minutes until tender. Drain and leave to cool.
4. Stir in the breadcrumbs, then the beaten eggs. Sprinkle with nutmeg, salt and pepper to taste.
5. Place half the greens mixture in the tin on top of the bacon. Lay the eggs down the centre and cover with the remaining greens mixture. Fold the overlapping bacon into the centre to enclose the filling.
6. Cover the tin with foil and bake in a preheated oven for 40 minutes until firm. Leave to cool. [A]
7. Turn out on to a serving dish and garnish with salad ingredients. Cut into 8 slices.

[A] Can be made up to 1 day ahead, covered and kept chilled.

*Variation:*
To convert it into a vegetarian salad, line the loaf tin with rinsed, preserved vine leaves rather than bacon rashers.

FROM THE LEFT: *Asparagus mousse salad; Spring green terrine*

# NUTTY STUFFED TOMATOES

*Serves 6*

6 large tomatoes
225 g (8 oz) cottage cheese
75 g (3 oz) salted peanuts, roughly chopped
1 tablespoon chopped fresh basil
50 g (2 oz) sultanas
3 spring onions, finely chopped
salt
freshly ground black pepper
lettuce leaves, to serve

*Preparation time: 30 minutes*

1. Cut the tops off the tomatoes and set aside. Hollow out the tomatoes, discarding the flesh and pips (these could be added to your stock pot).
2. Turn the cottage cheese into a bowl and add the peanuts, basil, sultanas and spring onions. Mix together well, then season to taste with salt and pepper.
3. Divide this mixture between the tomato shells, then replace the caps.
4. Serve garnished with lettuce leaves.

# WINTER ROOT SALAD

6 tablespoons orange juice
2 tablespoons wine vinegar
3 tablespoons oil
50 g (2 oz) raisins
225 g (8 oz) celeriac, peeled
225 g (8 oz) carrots, peeled
salt
freshly ground black pepper

*Preparation time: 20 minutes, plus marinating*

Remember that celeriac must be tossed in dressing as soon as it is peeled to prevent it turning brown.

1. Mix together the orange juice, vinegar and oil in a bowl. Add salt and pepper to taste, and the raisins.
2. Cut the celeriac and carrots into fine julienne strips and add to the orange dressing. Mix well until everything is thoroughly coated in dressing.
3. Cover and marinate for 1-2 hours before serving, tossing occasionally, to soften the celeriac. [A]

[A] Can be prepared up to 1 day ahead, covered and kept chilled.

FROM THE LEFT: *Winter root salad; Turnip and watercress salad; Winter leaf salad; Christmas coleslaw*

# TURNIP AND WATERCRESS SALAD

750 g (1½ lb) turnips
2 tablespoons lemon juice
salt
freshly ground black pepper
1 large bunch watercress, stalks removed
1 tablespoon Dijon mustard
150 ml (¼ pint) mayonnaise

*Preparation time: 15 minutes, plus marinating*

1. Peel the turnips and grate coarsely into long thin strips. Alternatively, cut into julienne strips with a knife.
2. Place the strips of turnip in a mixing bowl. Pour the lemon juice over and add salt and pepper to taste. Toss and leave to marinate for about 30 minutes to soften the turnip. [A]
3. Roughly chop the watercress and add to the strips of turnip.
4. Mix the mustard with the mayonnaise and add to the salad. Toss well to coat the turnip strips and watercress thoroughly.

[A] Can be prepared several hours in advance, covered and kept chilled.

# WINTER LEAF SALAD

½ head endive
1 large head chicory
1 head radiccio (red chicory)
1 bunch watercress
1 head celery leaves
*French dressing:*
2 tablespoons wine vinegar or lemon juice
6 tablespoons oil (olive, sunflower or walnut)
pinch of salt
freshly ground black pepper

*Preparation time: 15 minutes*

1. Separate the endive into individual leaves, keeping the stems intact, and place in a salad bowl.
2. Slice the chicory crosswise into thin rings and add to the endive.
3. Separate the radiccio leaves and add to the bowl.
4. Cut off the coarse watercress stalks and separate the celery leaves. Add the watercress and celery leaves to the salad.
5. Just before serving, whisk all the ingredients for the French dressing together thoroughly, pour over the salad and toss until all the leaves are well coated.

# CHRISTMAS COLESLAW

100 g (4 oz) red cabbage
100 g (4 oz) white cabbage
2 dessert apples, preferably red-skinned
50 g (2 oz) chopped nuts (e.g. walnuts, almonds, or brazils)
150 ml (¼ pint) mayonnaise
2 tablespoons French dressing (see left)
1 tablespoon chopped fresh parsley, to garnish

*Preparation time: 15 minutes*

1. Shred both the cabbages very thinly and place in a large bowl.
2. Cut the apples into quarters, remove the cores and cut into very thin slices, keeping the skins on, and add to the cabbage.
3. Add the chopped nuts.
4. Mix the mayonnaise with the French dressing. Pour over the cabbage salad and toss until everything is thoroughly coated. [A]
5. Transfer to a serving dish and garnish with the chopped fresh parsley.

[A] Can be prepared several hours in advance, covered and kept chilled.

# FENNEL AND APPLE SALAD

*Serves 4-6 as a side salad*

2 small bulbs fennel, about 450 g (1 lb)
4 small or 3 large dessert apples
50 g (2 oz) shelled hazelnuts, roughly chopped
150 ml (¼ pint) thick mayonnaise
5 tablespoons orange juice
salt
freshly ground black pepper

*Preparation time: 15 minutes*

1. Cut the fennel bulbs in half lengthways. Trim off the feathery green leaves from the tops and reserve for the garnish. Slice the fennel very finely and put in a large mixing bowl.
2. Quarter the apples, remove the cores, and cut into thin slices. Add the apples and chopped hazelnuts to the fennel.
3. Spoon the mayonnaise into a large bowl or jug, add the orange juice and blend until smooth. Add salt and pepper to taste.
4. Pour the dressing over the salad and toss until all the ingredients are thoroughly coated in dressing.
5. Garnish with the reserved fennel leaves. Serve as a side salad with cold roast meat or with whole, cold poached fish.

FROM THE LEFT: *Fennel and apple salad; Crunchy green salad with blue cheese dressing; Beef and radish salad*

# CRUNCHY GREEN SALAD WITH BLUE CHEESE DRESSING

*Serves 4-6 as a side salad*

100 g (4 oz) green cabbage, sliced thinly
100 g (4 oz) broccoli, divided into florets and sliced
100 g (4 oz) courgettes, sliced very thinly
1 small green pepper, halved, seeded and sliced very thinly
1 stick celery, thinly sliced
*Blue cheese dressing:*
150 ml (¼ pint) plain unsweetened yogurt
1 tablespoon white wine vinegar or lemon juice
salt
freshly ground black pepper
2 tablespoons crumbled blue cheese, e.g. Stilton, Danish blue, Roquefort

*Preparation time: 25 minutes*

1. Wash and drain all the vegetables, then place in a large salad bowl.
2. To make the dressing, beat together or liquidize the yogurt, vinegar or lemon juice and salt and stir in the cheese.
3. Pour the dressing over the vegetables and toss well. Leave to marinate for 1 hour before serving.

# BREAD AND CHEESE SALAD

4 thick slices day-old bread (brown or white),
weighing together about 100 g (4 oz)
1 quantity French dressing (page 13)
1 teaspoon fresh thyme leaves, or
½ teaspoon dried thyme
8 sticks celery, sliced crosswise
4 tomatoes, cut into wedges
225 g (8 oz) hard cheese, e.g. Lancashire,
Double Gloucester, Cheddar, Edam
lettuce or endive (optional)
celery leaves, to garnish

*Preparation time: 15 minutes*

1. Cut the bread into cubes, about 2 cm (¾ inch) square, and place in a large bowl.
2. Mix the French dressing with the thyme and pour over the bread. Toss until all the bread is coated in dressing.
3. Add the celery and tomatoes and toss lightly.
4. Cut the cheese into small cubes or sticks and add to the salad. [A]
5. Serve as a main salad straight from the bowl, or on a bed of lettuce or endive, garnished with celery leaves.

[A] Can be prepared several hours in advance, covered and kept chilled.

# BEEF AND RADISH SALAD

450 g (1 lb) cold rare roast beef
1 bunch radishes, with leaves
50 g (2 oz) walnut halves, broken
1 small endive (optional)
*Dressing:*
4 tablespoons walnut or olive oil
2 tablespoons orange juice
1 tablespoon wine vinegar
salt
freshly ground black pepper

*Preparation time: 15 minutes*

1. Thinly slice the beef and cut into strips about 4 × 1 cm (1½ × ½ inch) and place in a bowl.
2. Select a few of the best radishes to make 'roses' for garnishing: with a small, sharp knife make long incisions running from the top of each radish to within 1 cm (½ inch) of the base. Leave in iced water for several hours, or overnight, to open out. Thinly slice the remaining radishes and add to the beef.
3. Add the walnuts to the bowl.
4. Mix all the ingredients for the dressing together and pour over the ingredients in the bowl. Toss until everything is well coated in dressing. [A]
5. Arrange a bed of endive (if using) in a serving dish. Pile the beef and radish salad in the centre and garnish with the radish roses and radish leaves.

[A] Can be prepared several hours in advance, covered and kept chilled.

# CABBAGE BASKET

1 small white or green cabbage
salt
450 g (1 lb) carrots, scraped
50 g (2 oz) soft margarine
1 medium onion, peeled and chopped
1 garlic clove, peeled and crushed
1 teaspoon ground ginger
1 tablespoon clear honey
100 g (4 oz) cooked brown rice
100 g (4 oz) hazelnuts, chopped
freshly ground black pepper
40 g (1½ oz) fresh wholewheat breadcrumbs
1 hard-boiled egg, shelled and finely chopped
1 tablespoon chopped fresh parsley

*Preparation time: 1 hour*
*Cooking time: 1¾ hours*

1. Remove any damaged or discoloured outer leaves from the cabbage and trim to a neat shape. Blanch in boiling, salted water for 5 minutes. Drain thoroughly.
2. Cook the carrots in boiling, salted water for 10 minutes. Drain, reserving the liquid, and chop them finely.
3. Place the cabbage on a board. With 2 large spoons, gently pull a few leaves outwards, to expose the centre leaves and stalk. Remove these, leaving firm 'walls' about 2.5 cm (1 inch) thick. Finely chop the centre leaves.
4. Melt half the margarine and fry the onion and garlic over moderate heat for 3 minutes, stirring once or twice. Stir in the chopped cabbage, carrots, ginger, honey, rice, half the hazelnuts and 4 tablespoons of the reserved carrot stock. Season with salt and pepper, remove from the heat and stir well.
5. Pack the filling into the cabbage 'basket' and wrap it lightly in foil.
6. Stand the cabbage on a trivet in a pan of fast-boiling water, reduce the heat, cover the pan and cook for 1½ hours.
7. Melt the remaining margarine and fry the breadcrumbs and reserved nuts. Stir in the egg and parsley.
8. Transfer the cabbage to a heated serving dish and sprinkle the crumb mixture on top. Serve hot.

FROM THE LEFT: *Cabbage basket; Celery and walnut roll; Kitchen-garden loaf*

# KITCHEN-GARDEN LOAF

*Serves 6-8*

2 medium carrots, scraped and cut into matchsticks
175 g (6 oz) asparagus spears
175 g (6 oz) French beans, topped and tailed
salt
25 g (1 oz) soft margarine
1 medium onion, peeled and chopped
1 garlic clove, peeled and crushed
225 g (8 oz) button mushrooms, chopped (reserve 2 for garnish)
225 g (8 oz) cottage cheese
50 g (2 oz) Roquefort cheese, crumbled
4 eggs
150 ml (¼ pint) plain unsweetened yogurt
1 tablespoon chopped fresh parsley
½ teaspoon dried thyme
¼ teaspoon grated nutmeg
freshly ground black pepper
1 hard-boiled egg, shelled and sliced, to garnish

*Dressing:*
150 ml (¼ pint) plain unsweetened yogurt
1 teaspoon French mustard
½ teaspoon curry powder
2 tablespoons double cream
1 teaspoon lemon juice

*Preparation time: 45 minutes*
*Cooking time: 1¾ hours*
*Oven: 180°C, 350°F, Gas Mark 4*

1. Cook the carrots, asparagus and beans in boiling, salted water until they are just tender. Drain and plunge at once into cold water to prevent further cooking. Drain again. Pat dry.
2. Grease a 1 kg (2 lb) loaf tin and line it with greased greaseproof paper.
3. Melt the margarine and gently fry the onion and garlic for 3 minutes, stirring. Add the mushrooms and cook for 3 minutes.
4. Blend the onion mixture with the cheese, eggs, yogurt and parsley until smooth. Add the thyme and nutmeg and season.
5. Pour one quarter of the egg and cheese mixture

into the prepared tin. Lay the asparagus spears over them lengthways along the tin. Pour in one third of the remaining mixture and top with a layer of carrots. Pour on one half of the remaining mixture, top with a layer of beans then pour on the rest of the mixture.
6. Stand in a roasting tin half filled with water. Cover with foil. Place in a preheated oven and bake for 1½ hours, or until the egg custard is set. Cool the tin on a wire rack, then chill.
7. Turn the loaf out on to a plate. Garnish with slices of egg and the reserved mushrooms. Leave at room temperature for 30 minutes.
8. To make the dressing, mix all the ingredients together and serve chilled.

# CELERY AND WALNUT ROLL

4 eggs, separated
75 g (3 oz) Gruyère cheese, grated
2 teaspoons celery seed
4 tablespoons celery leaves, finely chopped
*Filling:*
175 g (6 oz) low fat soft cheese
75 g (3 oz) walnuts, chopped
2 tablespoons chopped flat-leaved parsley
freshly ground black pepper
celery leaves, to garnish

*Preparation time: 25 minutes*
*Cooking time: 30 minutes*
*Oven: 200°C, 400°F, Gas Mark 6*

1. Line a Swiss roll tin with greased greaseproof paper.
2. Beat the egg yolks until they are creamy, then beat in 25 g (1 oz) of the cheese, the celery seed and celery leaves.
3. Whisk the egg whites until stiff and fold them into the celery mixture. Spread the mixture over the prepared tin and level the top.
4. Place in a preheated oven and bake for 25 minutes, or until firm to the touch.
5. Beat together the soft cheese, walnuts and parsley and season with pepper.
6. Remove the tin from the oven. Spread the filling over the sponge base and, using the paper to lift it up, roll it up from one short end.
7. Lift the roll on to a heatproof dish. Sprinkle the remaining cheese on top and return it to the oven for 3-4 minutes to melt the cheese. Serve hot.

# SOUFFLÉ COURGETTES

6 medium courgettes
salt
350 g (12 oz) tomatoes, skinned and sliced
1 teaspoon dried oregano
freshly ground black pepper
1 tablespoon tomato purée
1 teaspoon lemon juice
2 eggs, separated
1 egg white
75 g (3 oz) Gruyère cheese, grated
pinch of cayenne

*Preparation time: 20 minutes*
*Cooking time: 1 hour*
*Oven: 180°C, 350°F, Gas Mark 4*

1. Cook the courgettes in boiling, salted water for 5 minutes. Drain and cut off the ends. Slice the courgettes in half lengthways and scoop out the flesh, leaving firm 'walls'. Chop the flesh. Leave to cool.
2. Put the tomatoes, oregano, pepper, tomato purée and lemon juice into a pan, stir well and bring to the boil.
3. Beat the egg yolks and chopped courgette flesh together. Whisk the egg whites and fold into the egg yolk mixture with 50 g (2 oz) of the cheese, salt, pepper and cayenne.
4. Spoon the tomato sauce into a baking dish. Arrange the courgette halves on top, cut sides up, and spoon the soufflé mixture into the 'shells'. Sprinkle over the remaining cheese.
5. Place in a preheated oven and bake the courgettes for 35 minutes, or until the cheese mixture is well risen and firm. Serve at once.

ABOVE: *Soufflé courgettes*
RIGHT: *Vegetable cobbler*

# VEGETABLE COBBLER

*Serves 6*

3 medium carrots, scraped and thinly sliced
½ small cauliflower, divided into florets
salt
50 g (2 oz) soft margarine
8 small leeks, thickly sliced
2 small heads fennel, sliced
25 g (1 oz) wholewheat flour
450 ml (¾ pint) chicken stock
freshly ground black pepper
2 tablespoons chopped fresh parsley
*Topping:*
175 g (6 oz) wholewheat flour
1 teaspoon bicarbonate of soda
salt
75 g (3 oz) oat flakes
40 g (1½ oz) soft margarine
1 large egg
3 tablespoons plain unsweetened yogurt
50 g (2 oz) Edam cheese, grated

*Preparation time: 45 minutes*
*Cooking time: 1¼ hours,*
*Oven: 180°C, 350°F, Gas Mark 4;*
*then: 200°C, 400°F, Gas Mark 6*

1. Cook the carrots and cauliflower in boiling, salted water for 5 minutes. Drain and place in a casserole.
2. Melt half the margarine and fry the leeks and fennel over moderate heat for 4 minutes, stirring frequently. Transfer to the casserole.
3. Melt the remaining margarine, stir in the flour and cook for 1 minute. Remove the pan from the heat and gradually stir in the stock. Season with salt and pepper and bring to the boil. Simmer for 3 minutes. Stir in the parsley and pour the sauce over the vegetables.
4. Cover the casserole and place in a preheated oven for 45 minutes.
5. Sift the flour, soda and salt together and tip the bran from the sieve back into the bowl. Add half the oat flakes and mix in the margarine. Beat in the egg and yogurt to make a firm dough. Shape the dough into a ball and knead lightly until it is smooth.
6. Roll out the dough on a lightly-floured board to 1 cm/½ inch thick and cut into rounds with a biscuit cutter.
7. Arrange the rounds on the vegetables, sprinkle with the cheese mixed with the remaining oat flakes. Increase the oven temperature and bake for 15 minutes, or until the topping is golden. Garnish with fennel fronds. Serve at once.

# BROCCOLI IN WHOLEGRAIN MUSTARD SAUCE

450 g (1 lb) broccoli, cut into florets
salt
15 g (½ oz) butter
15 g (½ oz) plain flour
200 ml (7 fl oz) milk
2 teaspoons wholegrain mustard
½ teaspoon lemon juice
freshly ground black pepper
15 g (½ oz) toasted flaked almonds, to garnish

*Preparation time: 10 minutes*
*Cooking time: 30-40 minutes*
*Oven: 180°C, 350°F, Gas Mark 4*

1. Put the broccoli into a pan of boiling, salted water, bring to the boil and simmer for 3 minutes. Drain well, then put the broccoli into a casserole.
2. Melt the butter in a pan, add the flour and cook for 1 minute. Gradually add the milk, bring to the boil and simmer for 2-3 minutes. Add the mustard, lemon juice and pepper, then pour over the broccoli.
3. Cover the casserole, put into a preheated oven and cook for 20-30 minutes until the broccoli is tender.
4. Serve the casserole garnished with toasted flaked almonds.

# SCALLOPED CABBAGE

750 g (1½ lb) white cabbage, shredded
1 large onion, peeled and sliced
6 juniper berries, crushed
salt
75 g (3 oz) butter
25 g (1 oz) plain flour
300 ml (½ pint) milk
freshly ground black pepper
100 g (4 oz) fresh white breadcrumbs

*Preparation time: 20 minutes*
*Cooking time: 1 hour*
*Oven: 180°C, 350°F, Gas Mark 4*

There are many varieties of cabbage available according to the time of year, and this recipe may be prepared using one of the other varieties or another green vegetable, such as spinach (when a garlic clove could be substituted for the juniper berries), broccoli florets or chopped Brussels sprouts.

The recipe makes a very good vegetable accompaniment. To serve as a more substantial main course add some cheese or chopped nuts to the final layer. Serve with potatoes, either baked or boiled in their skins, and carrots.

1. Put the cabbage, onion and juniper berries into a pan of boiling, salted water, bring back to the boil and simmer for 5 minutes. Drain well, reserving 150 ml (¼ pint) of the cooking water.
2. Melt 25 g (1 oz) of the butter in a pan, add the flour and cook for 1 minute. Gradually add the milk, cabbage water and pepper, bring to the boil and cook for 3 minutes, then add to the cabbage and mix well. [A]
3. Melt the remaining butter in a frying pan, add the breadcrumbs and fry until lightly browned. [A]
4. Put a third of the cabbage into a casserole and sprinkle with two tablespoons of the breadcrumbs, repeat the layers, then cover the top with the remaining breadcrumbs.
5. Put into a preheated oven and cook for 40 minutes, until the topping is golden brown.

[A] The cabbage and breadcrumbs can be prepared up to 8 hours in advance. Proceed as in the recipe.

# BAKED CUCUMBER IN COTTAGE CHEESE SAUCE

25 g (1 oz) butter
1½ large cucumbers,
peeled, seeded and diced
1 × 225 g (8 oz) pack cottage cheese with chives
2 tablespoons double or whipping cream
1 teaspoon chopped fresh dill or ½ teaspoon
dried dillweed
salt
freshly ground black pepper

CLOCKWISE FROM TOP: *Broccoli in wholegrain mustard sauce; Scalloped cabbage; Baked cucumber in cottage cheese sauce*

*Preparation time: 10 minutes*
*Cooking time: 35 minutes*
*Oven: 180°C, 350°F, Gas Mark 4*

1. Melt the butter in a flameproof casserole, add the cucumber and stir around until the cucumber is coated with the butter.
2. Add the cottage cheese, cream, dill, salt and pepper, bring to the boil, cover the casserole and put into a preheated oven. Cook for about 30 minutes until the cucumber is tender.

21

# BAKED RATATOUILLE WITH GOAT'S CHEESE CROÛTES

2 tablespoons olive oil
1 large onion, peeled and sliced
2 garlic cloves, peeled and crushed
1 red pepper, cored, seeded and sliced
1 green pepper, cored, seeded and sliced
225 g (8 oz) aubergine, stalk removed and diced
225 g (8 oz) courgettes, topped, tailed and sliced
1 × 400 g (14 oz) can chopped tomatoes
2 teaspoons Herbes de Provence
salt
freshly ground black pepper
1 small French loaf
2-3 tablespoons oil
175-225 g (6-8 oz) goat's cheese, cut into 8

*Preparation time: 20 minutes*
*Cooking time: 1 hour 20 minutes*
*Oven: 180°C, 350°F, Gas Mark 4*

1. Heat the oil in a flameproof casserole, add the onion and garlic and cook until soft. Add the peppers, aubergine and courgettes to the casserole and mix well, then add the tomatoes and juice, Herbes de Provence, salt and pepper. Bring to the boil, cover the casserole and put into a preheated oven and cook for 1 hour. [A] [F]
2. After the casserole has been in the oven for 45 minutes, cut the French loaf into 8 slices, about 2.5-3 cm (1-1½ inches) wide, discarding the ends.
3. Dip each slice of the French bread into the oil, place on a baking sheet and put into the oven above the casserole for 15 minutes until crisp.
4. Take the casserole from the oven, remove the lid, stir the vegetables, then put the slices of bread on top of the vegetables. Put a piece of goat's cheese on top of each piece of French bread. Put under a preheated hot grill until the cheese is bubbling.

[A] The ratatouille can be prepared 1 day in advance. Keep covered and chilled, then proceed with the recipe.

[F] Freeze for up to 3 months. Defrost for 4-6 hours at room temperature or overnight in a refrigerator. Reheat for 30 minutes at 180°C, 350°F, Gas Mark 4.

FROM THE TOP: *Baked ratatouille with goat's cheese croûtes; Chicory casserole with toasted walnuts; Courgette and brown rice layered casserole*

# CHICORY CASSEROLE WITH TOASTED WALNUTS

8 small, even-sized heads of chicory, approx. 100 g
(4 oz) each
salt
2 tablespoons lemon juice
25 g (1 oz) butter
1 small onion, peeled and finely chopped
1 tablespoon plain flour
85 ml (3 fl oz) milk
150 ml (5 fl oz) vegetable stock
freshly ground black pepper
50 g (2 oz) chopped walnuts

*Preparation time: 15 minutes*
*Cooking time: 1 hour–1 hour 10 minutes*
*Oven: 180°C, 350°F, Gas Mark 4*

1. Remove the core from the base of each chicory head and discard. Put the chicory into a pan of boiling, salted water with 1 tablespoon of the lemon juice and cook for 5 minutes. (The lemon juice prevents the chicory heads turning brown when cooked.) Drain well, then put into a shallow casserole.
2. Melt the butter in a pan, add the onion and cook for 2 minutes. Stir in the flour and cook for a further minute. Gradually add the milk and vegetable stock to the pan, bring to the boil and cook for 2-3 minutes. Add the pepper and remaining lemon juice, then pour over the chicory.
3. Cover the casserole and cook in a preheated oven for 30-40 minutes, until the chicory is tender.
4. Put the walnuts on to a baking sheet and put them into the oven at the same time as the chicory, taking them out again after about 10 minutes.
5. Serve the chicory sprinkled with the toasted walnuts.

# COURGETTE AND BROWN RICE LAYERED CASSEROLE

2 tablespoons oil
1 onion, peeled and chopped
1 garlic clove, peeled and crushed
225 g (8 oz) tomatoes, peeled, seeded and chopped
450 g (1 lb) courgettes, topped, tailed and
thinly sliced
½ teaspoon dried tarragon
salt
freshly ground black pepper
450 g (1 lb) cooked brown rice
2 eggs, beaten
150 ml (5 fl oz) double or whipping cream
100 g (4 oz) grated Cheddar cheese

*Preparation time: 20 minutes*
*Cooking time: 50 minutes*
*Oven: 180°C, 350°F, Gas Mark 4*

1. Heat the oil in a pan, add the onion and garlic and cook until soft. Add the tomatoes, courgettes, tarragon, salt and pepper and cook for a further 3-4 minutes. Ⓐ
2. Mix together the rice, eggs, cream, most of the cheese and a little salt and pepper. Ⓐ
3. Put a third of the rice mixture into a casserole followed by half of the courgette mixture. Repeat, then finish with a layer of rice. Sprinkle the remaining cheese over the top. Place in a preheated oven and cook for 40 minutes.

Ⓐ The courgettes and rice can be prepared up to 8 hours in advance, then proceed with the recipe.

# SPINACH VINAIGRETTE

750 g (1½ lb) young spinach
salt
40 g (1½ oz) pine nuts, or blanched,
slivered almonds
1 small onion, peeled and thinly sliced
into rings (optional)
lemon slices, to serve
*Dressing:*
4 tablespoons olive oil
1 tablespoon lemon juice
2 tablespoons chopped mint
freshly ground black pepper
½ teaspoon soft light brown sugar

*Preparation time: 15 minutes*
*Cooking time: 5 minutes*

1. Wash the spinach and cook in the water clinging
   to the leaves with a pinch of salt in a large pan for 5
   minutes or until tender. Drain in a colander,
   gently pressing out the water without damaging
   any of the leaves.
2. Mix all the dressing ingredients together.
3. Mix the spinach in the dressing and stir in the pine
   nuts. Serve just warm or cool – but not chilled.
   Garnish with the onion rings, if liked, and serve
   with lemon slices.

# POTATO AND PARSNIP LAYER

*Serves 6*

450 g (1 lb) potatoes, peeled and cut into 5 mm
(¼ inch) slices
1 large onion, peeled and thinly sliced into rings
225 g (8 oz) parsnips, peeled and cut into 5 mm
(¼ inch) slices
25 g (1 oz) soft margarine
salt
freshly ground black pepper
pinch of grated nutmeg
300 ml (½ pint) milk or buttermilk

*Preparation time: 20 minutes*
*Cooking time: 2 hours*
*Oven: 180°C, 350°F, Gas Mark 4*

1. Make layers of potato, onion and parsnip in a
   well-greased baking dish. Dot the potatoes with
   margarine and season each layer with salt, pepper
   and nutmeg, finishing with a layer of potatoes.
   Pour the milk over.
2. Stand the dish on a baking sheet and cover with a
   lid or foil. Place in a preheated oven and bake for 2
   hours. Remove the covering for the last 30 minutes to brown the potatoes. Serve hot.

# ARTICHOKE NESTS

750 g (1½ lb) Jerusalem artichokes
1 tablespoon lemon juice
150 ml (¼ pint) chicken stock
25 g (1 oz) soft margarine
4 tablespoons milk
salt
freshly ground black pepper
pinch of grated nutmeg
1 tablespoon chopped fresh mint
1 egg
25 g (1 oz) ground almonds

*Preparation time: 40 minutes*
*Cooking time: 35 minutes*
*Oven: 180°C, 350°F, Gas Mark 4*

1. Peel the artichokes and immediately drop them
   into a small bowl of water, acidulated with the
   lemon juice to preserve the colour.
2. Cook the artichokes in the stock for 15 minutes or
   until tender.
3. Drain and mash them with the margarine, milk,
   salt, pepper, nutmeg and mint. Beat in the egg and
   almonds. Beat to make a smooth thick paste. Cool
   slightly.
4. Using a piping bag and large round nozzle, pipe
   the artichoke paste on to a greased baking sheet to
   make 4 round 'nests'.
5. Place in a preheated oven and bake for 20 minutes, or until firm. Fill the nests with cooked vegetables of your choice.

CLOCKWISE FROM THE TOP: *Spinach vinaigrette; Potato and parsnip layer; Artichoke nests*

# VEGETABLE MOUSSAKA

100 g (4 oz) brown 'continental' lentils, soaked
overnight and drained
450 g (1 lb) tomatoes, skinned and chopped
1 teaspoon dried oregano
1 bay leaf
1 teaspoon soft dark brown sugar
salt
freshly ground black pepper
sunflower oil, for frying
1 large aubergine, thinly sliced
450 g (1 lb) potatoes, peeled and thinly sliced
*Sauce:*
25 g (1 oz) soft margarine
25 g (1 oz) wholewheat flour
300 ml (½ pint) milk
150 ml (¼ pint) plain unsweetened yogurt
100 g (4 oz) Feta, crumbled, or Wensleydale
cheese, grated
1 egg
large pinch of grated nutmeg

*Preparation time: 30 minutes, plus overnight soaking*
*Cooking time: 2½ hours*
*Oven: 190°C, 375°F, Gas Mark 5*

1. Cook the lentils in boiling, unsalted water for 1
   hour. Drain.
2. Simmer the tomatoes with the bay leaf, oregano,
   sugar, salt and pepper for 20 minutes.
3. Mix the lentils into the tomato mixture and simmer for 10 minutes, stirring, until thick.
4. Heat the oil and fry the aubergine slices a few at a
   time over moderate heat until they begin to
   colour.
5. Cook the potato slices in boiling, salted water for
   10 minutes, or until they begin to soften.
6. Make layers of the tomato and lentil sauce, aubergines and potatoes in a greased casserole, finishing with potatoes.
7. Melt the margarine and stir in the flour. Cook for
   1 minute, then remove the pan from the heat.
   Gradually stir in the milk, then the yogurt. Bring
   to the boil, then simmer for 3 minutes. Remove
   from the heat. Beat in half of the cheese, and the
   egg and season with salt, pepper and nutmeg.
8. Pour the sauce over the dish and sprinkle the
   remaining cheese on top.
9. Stand the casserole on a baking sheet. Place in a
   preheated oven and bake for 35-40 minutes, or
   until the sauce is bubbling and browned.

# ASPARAGUS QUICHE

*Serves 6*
175 g (6 oz) wholewheat self-raising flour
salt
50 g (2 oz) white vegetable fat
25 g (1 oz) butter
40 g (1½oz) cottage cheese, sieved
*½-1 teaspoon fennel seeds, lightly crushed*
*Filling:*
350 g (12 oz) asparagus spears, cooked and drained
75 g (3 oz) low fat soft cheese
150 ml (¼ pint) plain unsweetened yogurt
6 tablespoons milk
2 eggs
freshly ground black pepper

*Preparation time: 25 minutes, plus chilling*
*Cooking time: 1 hour*
*Oven: 190°C, 375°F, Gas Mark 5*

1. Sift the flour and salt together and tip the bran from the sieve back into the bowl. Rub in the fats until the mixture is like fine breadcrumbs. Stir in the cheese and fennel and mix to a dough with a very little cold water. Knead the dough lightly. Wrap in clingfilm or foil and chill for at least 30 minutes.
2. Roll out the pastry on a lightly floured board and use to line a greased 20 cm (8 inch) flan ring on a greased baking sheet.
3. Arrange the asparagus spears in a wheel pattern in the pastry case.
4. Mix the cheese, yogurt and milk together, beat in the eggs and season with salt and pepper. Pour the filling into the pastry case.
5. Place in a preheated oven and bake for 40-45 minutes, until the filling is set. F Serve warm.

F Freeze for up to 2 months. Reheat from frozen in the oven for about 30 minutes.

# FRUITY AUBERGINE BOATS

4 aubergines, about 175 g (6 oz) each
salt
5 tablespoons sunflower oil
1 large onion, peeled and chopped
2 garlic cloves, peeled and finely chopped
450 g (1 lb) tomatoes, skinned and sliced
75 g (3 oz) sultanas
50 g (2 oz) seedless raisins
75 g (3 oz) blanched, slivered almonds
2 tablespoons chopped fresh parsley
½ teaspoon dried thyme
freshly ground black pepper
flat-leaved parsley, to garnish

*Preparation time: 25 minutes, plus salting*
*Cooking time: 1¼ hours*
*Oven: 180°C, 350°F, Gas Mark 4*

1. Cut off the stalk ends of the aubergines and halve them lengthways. Scoop out the flesh (a curved grapefruit knife is ideal for this), leaving firm 'walls'. Chop the aubergine flesh finely and put it in a colander. Sprinkle liberally with salt and leave for about 1 hour, to degorge (draw off the bitter juices).
2. Rinse the aubergine flesh in cold water and drain thoroughly on kitchen paper.
3. Heat the oil and fry the onion, garlic and aubergine flesh over a moderate heat for 5 minutes, stirring frequently.
4. Add the tomatoes, stir well and fry for a further 5 minutes.
5. Stir in the sultanas, raisins, almonds, parsley and thyme and season with salt and pepper.
6. Stand the aubergine shells cut side up in a greased baking dish and fill them with the tomato mixture.
7. Place in a preheated oven and bake the aubergines for 1 hour. Serve hot, garnished with the parsley leaves.

CLOCKWISE FROM THE LEFT: *Vegetable moussaka; Fruity aubergine boats; Asparagus quiche*

## CHAPTER TWO

# RIVER, SEA AND MOOR

This chapter features dishes using ingredients from the wild creatures of the countryside, be it fur, feather or fin. Many of the dishes are classics which come from those areas of the country where the fish or game are traditionally caught, from Wales up to Scotland or from the West country across to East Anglia. Some of the fish recipes are perfect for quick meals, whereas the game generally takes longer, but dishes such as casseroles can conveniently be left to cook themselves.

FROM THE TOP: *Fisherman's stew from the Gower peninsula; Trout wrapped in bacon*

# FISHERMAN'S STEW FROM THE GOWER PENINSULA

*Serves 6*

1.2 litres (2 pints) cockles,
scrubbed and soaked in cold water
3 medium onions
1 bouquet garni
½ teaspoon ground mace
salt
freshly ground black pepper
300 ml (½ pint) white wine
450 g (1 lb) haddock fillets, skinned
450 g (1 lb) plaice fillets, skinned
50 g (2 oz) butter
50 g (2 oz) plain flour
225 g (8 oz) crab meat
225 g (8 oz) shrimps
or prawns, shelled
1 teaspoon powdered saffron

*Preparation time: 20 minutes, plus soaking*
*Cooking time: 1 hour 20 minutes*

1. Strain the cockles, put in a large pan with 1.75 litres (3 pints) of water and bring to the boil. As soon as they open, take the pan from the heat and reserve the liquor. Using a teaspoon, remove the cockles from the shell, and set aside.
2. Strain the cooking liquor and add one of the onions, peeled and quartered, the bouquet garni, mace and a little salt and pepper. Bring to the boil, and reduce by one third by boiling briskly for 30 minutes.
3. Add the white wine and the remaining onions, peeled and finely chopped, to the broth.
4. Slide the haddock fillets into the liquid over the onions, then the plaice fillets on top of all.
5. Poach very gently for 30 minutes, then lift out the plaice fillets with a fish slice, cut each one in half and keep warm. Take out the haddock fillets, flake the flesh and set on one side.
6. Melt the butter in a large pan, add the flour and cook, stirring well for 2 minutes. Slowly stir the broth into it and simmer for 5 minutes until it thickens.
7. Return the flaked haddock to the broth, add the crab meat, the shrimps or prawns, the cockles and the saffron. Simmer for 2-3 minutes and adjust the seasoning as necessary.
8. Return the plaice fillets to the pan and serve immediately.

# Baked salmon

*Serves 6*

1 salmon, about 2 kg (4½ lb), cleaned
1 tablespoon flour
salt
freshly ground black pepper
50 g (2 oz) butter
1 sprig fresh tarragon
1 bay leaf
*Green butter:*
1 spinach leaf
3 sprigs fresh parsley
2 sprigs fresh mint
2 fresh sage leaves (optional)
75 g (3 oz) butter
pinch of salt

*Preparation time: 35 minutes, plus chilling*
*Cooking time: 35-45 minutes*
*Oven: 180°C, 350°F, Gas Mark 4*

1. To make the green butter, finely chop the spinach and fresh herbs, or pass them together through a parsley chopper. Mix the chopped herbs into the butter with a wooden spoon, beating well. Add the salt and form into a sausage shape. Chill for at least 1 hour.
2. Sprinkle the salmon inside and out with the flour, salt and pepper.
3. Butter a large sheet of foil and lay the salmon on it. Put the herbs on the fish and dot with the rest of the butter. Wrap up firmly.
4. Lay the parcel on a baking tray and bake in a pre-heated oven for 30-35 minutes. Open the parcel and insert a skewer to see if the fish is cooked. If not, cook for another 10 minutes.
5. When cooked, unwrap the fish and lay it on a flat, ovenproof dish. Cut slices of the chilled green butter and place along the fish. Return it to the oven for 2 minutes. Serve at once. The butter should be running down the sides of the salmon.

# Trout wrapped in bacon

This way of cooking trout has been traditional on Welsh farms for three hundred years and probably much longer.

50 g (2 oz) butter
4 medium trout, cleaned
2 sprigs fresh tarragon, chopped
2 sprigs fresh marjoram, chopped
4 tablespoons finely chopped onions or chives
1 teaspoon freshly ground black pepper
8 long rashers smoked streaky bacon
2 tablespoons finely chopped fresh parsley

*Preparation time: 10 minutes*
*Cooking time: 8-10 minutes*

1. Put a quarter of the butter in the cavity of each fish and press into it a quarter of the chopped herbs except the parsley and a quarter of the onions. Sprinkle ¼ teaspoon of black pepper into each.
2. Using scissors, cut the rind from the bacon rashers. Wind 2 rashers spirally round each fish, starting where the head joins the body and finishing at the tail fin.
3. Lay the fish on a grill pan, heads facing the same way, and cook under a pre-heated, very hot grill for 3-4 minutes. If the bacon begins to burn, lower the pan a little, but not the heat. After 3 minutes turn the trout and cook 3 minutes on the other side. Test with a skewer for doneness.
4. Serve sprinkled with chopped parsley.

*Baked salmon*

# BAKED RED MULLET IN PORT WINE

75 g (3 oz) butter
1 tablespoon finely chopped fresh parsley
1 tablespoon finely chopped shallot
4 red mullet, cleaned
1 teaspoon anchovy sauce
2 teaspoons Worcestershire sauce
350 ml (12 fl oz) port
40 g (1½ oz) flour
225 g (8 oz) tomatoes, stewed in 300 ml (½ pint)
water, then sieved
1 tablespoon double cream
1 tablespoon milk
salt
freshly ground black pepper

*Preparation time: 15 minutes*
*Cooking time: 30 minutes*
*Oven: 180°C, 350°F, Gas Mark 4*

1. Butter a shallow baking dish with 1 oz (25 g) of the butter, and sprinkle with half the parsley and shallot. Lay on the mullet and sprinkle the remainder of the parsley and shallot over them. Pour in the anchovy and Worcestershire sauces and the port.
2. Cover with foil and bake in a preheated oven for 15 minutes, then uncover and bake for a further 10-15 minutes.
3. While the fish is baking, make a roux with the remaining butter and the flour. Stir in the puréed tomatoes, the cream and enough milk to give the consistency of very thick cream. Season well and keep warm until the fish are done.
4. Lift the fish on to a warmed serving dish and pour the liquid from the baking dish into the sauce, stirring well.
5. Pour the sauce over the mullet and serve.

*Baked red mullet in port wine*

*Fish dinner from Yarmouth*

# FISH DINNER FROM YARMOUTH

*Serves 6*

50 g (2 oz) butter
2 large onions, peeled and finely chopped
3 mackerel, cleaned and filleted
1 teaspoon ground mace
½ teaspoon turmeric
salt
freshly ground black pepper
750 g (1½ lb) haddock, hake or cod fillets
900 ml (1½ pints) cold water
225 g (8 oz) crab meat
3 tablespoons chopped fresh parsley

*Preparation time: 10 minutes*
*Cooking time: 25 minutes*

1. Melt the butter in a large pan and fry the onions until just soft but not coloured.
2. Lay the fillets of mackerel on top of the onions and sprinkle with half the spices and a pinch of salt and pepper.
3. Add the haddock, hake or cod fillets and sprinkle on the remaining spices. Pour on the cold water. Bring to the boil and simmer very gently for 20 minutes.
4. Lift out the fish fillets and the onion with a perforated spoon, reserving the cooking liquid.
5. Arrange the fish in a large, shallow, ovenproof dish. (It does not matter if some pieces are broken.) Flake the crab meat and spread it on top of the fish.
6. Pour a little of the cooking liquid around and over the fish. Cover with foil and keep hot.
7. Adjust the seasoning of the remaining stock and serve in bowls with crusty bread, followed by the fish, thickly sprinkled with parsley and served with boiled potatoes with butter.

# HAKE WITH LEMON BUTTER SAUCE

4 thick hake cutlets
*Court bouillon:*
white fish heads, bones and skin
1 small onion, chopped
1 teaspoon grated lemon rind
6 black peppercorns
sprig of fresh parsley or fennel
900 ml (1½ pints) water,
or half white wine and half water
*Sauce:*
175 g (6 oz) butter
2 tablespoons cornflour
2 tablespoons lemon juice
salt
freshly ground black pepper
lemon twist
sprig of fennel

*Preparation time: 15 minutes*
*Cooking time: 45 minutes*

1. First make the court bouillon by putting the fish heads, bones and skin into a saucepan with all the other ingredients. Boil up, simmer for half an hour, then strain. Reserve the liquid.
2. Poach the hake cutlets in the court bouillon for about 10 minutes. Lift out and keep warm.
3. To make the sauce, melt the butter, then add the cornflour, mixing quickly.
4. Heat to thicken slightly, stirring all the time, then add the lemon juice and mix well. Season to taste.
5. Serve the sauce with the hake, pouring a little of it over before serving. Garnish with a lemon twist and a sprig of fennel.

# BUTTERED CRAB

450 g (1 lb) fresh or frozen crab meat
2 anchovy fillets
150 ml (¼ pint) dry white wine
pinch of grated nutmeg or mace
4 tablespoons fresh white breadcrumbs
salt
freshly ground black pepper
75 g (3 oz) butter
4 slices hot crustless buttered toast

FROM THE LEFT: *Hake with lemon butter sauce; Buttered crab; Herrings marinated and baked in tea*

*Preparation time: 15 minutes*
*Cooking time: 15 minutes*

1. Flake the crab meat coarsely.
2. Pound up the anchovies in the wine, add the nutmeg, breadcrumbs and seasonings. Put into a saucepan and bring gently to the boil, then simmer for about 3 minutes.
3. Mix the flaked crab meat with the butter and add to the hot wine mixture, stir and cook gently for 4 minutes.
4. Serve the crab with fingers of hot buttered toast.

# Herrings marinated and baked in tea

This is an excellent West Country method of pickling fish. Mackerel, sprats or pilchards can be cooked in this way.

8 herrings, cleaned
8 bay leaves
1 tablespoon brown sugar
15 whole black peppercorns
150 ml (¼ pint) white vinegar
150 ml (¼ pint) cold, milkless tea

*Preparation time: 30 minutes*
*Cooking time: 1 hour*
*Oven: 180°C, 350°F, Gas Mark 4*

1. Lay the fish in an ovenproof dish and put a bay leaf, crumbled, into each one. Sprinkle evenly with the brown sugar and peppercorns.
2. Combine the vinegar and tea, then pour the mixture over the fish so that they are barely covered.
3. Cover loosely with foil and bake in the preheated oven for about 1 hour.
4. Leave to get cold in the liquor, which will jell slightly. Serve a little of the jelly with each portion.

# BAKED SEA TROUT

This fish is often referred to as salmon trout because the flesh is pink, but it is considered by many people to be more delicately flavoured. The finest of all are caught in the sea lochs of Scotland.

*Serves 4-6*

1 sea trout, about 750 g (1¾ lb), cleaned
15 g (½ oz) butter
2 teaspoons plain flour
salt
freshly ground black pepper
1 teaspoon lemon juice
1 sprig each fresh parsley, fennel, marjoram and tarragon or 1 bouquet garni
*To garnish:*
½ cucumber, finely sliced
sprigs of fennel and tarragon

*Preparation time: 5 minutes*
*Cooking time: 35 minutes*
*Oven: 200°C, 400°F, Gas Mark 6*

1. Spread out a piece of foil large enough to wrap up the fish well. Butter it well and sprinkle with flour, salt and pepper. Lay the fish in the centre.
2. Rub the inside of the fish with salt and pepper, sprinkle in the lemon juice and add the fresh herbs, if available.
3. Wrap up the fish, making a close parcel that will keep the juices in. Lay on a baking sheet and bake in a preheated oven for 30 minutes.
4. Remove from the oven and undo the parcel, allowing the juice to run into the baking sheet. Lift the fish very carefully, supporting it at both ends so that it does not break, on to a hot, ovenproof dish.
5. Strain the juice and pour it over. Put the fish back into the oven for 4 minutes, so that the top of the skin is slightly crisped.
6. Serve with slices of cucumber and sprigs of fresh herbs arranged round it.

# ARBROATH SMOKIES

Arbroath smokies are small haddock, lightly smoked. They have a fine flavour and texture and can be found in most good fishmongers.

4 Arbroath smokies
150 ml (¼ pint) single cream
freshly ground black pepper
watercress sprigs, to garnish

*Preparation time: 3 minutes*
*Cooking time: 10 minutes*

1. Bring enough water to boil in a frying pan just to cover the smokies. Put the fish in and simmer for 5 minutes.
2. Lift out the smokies and drain. Pour off the water from the pan. Return the smokies to the pan and pour the cream over them.
3. Simmer very gently, shaking the pan and turning the smokies over for 5 minutes, or until quite tender.
4. Lift the fish on to a serving dish, and pour the creamy sauce from the pan over them. Sprinkle with black pepper and garnish with watercress.

# HERRINGS IN OATMEAL

*Serves 6*

6 herrings, filleted
salt
freshly ground black pepper
75-100 g (3-4 oz) coarse oatmeal
100 g (4 oz) butter or melted bacon fat
1 tablespoon chopped fresh parsley
1 lemon, thinly sliced

*Preparation time: 5 minutes*
*Cooking time: 10 minutes*

1. Rub the herring fillets with salt and pepper.
2. Sprinkle the oatmeal evenly on a board or plate and press both sides of the herrings well into it. It will adhere to the oily surface of the fish.
3. Put the butter or bacon fat into a frying pan and heat until it is just sizzling. Fry the herrings for about 3 minutes on each side, or until they are golden brown and crisp.
4. Lift from the pan on to a hot dish, sprinkle the parsley over the fillets and arrange the lemon slices round the edge. Serve immediately, while hot, as a breakfast or supper dish.

FROM THE BOTTOM, CLOCKWISE: *Arbroath smokies; Baked sea trout; Herrings in oatmeal*

# GAME PIE

25 g (1 oz) butter
1 large onion, peeled and finely chopped
2 partridges or 1 other small game bird or 1
pheasant, cleaned and jointed
225 g (8 oz) lean steak,
cut into 2.5 cm (1 inch) pieces
2 rashers bacon,
rinded and cut into 1 cm (½ inch) strips
100 g (4 oz) mushrooms, cleaned
1 sprig fresh thyme
1 bay leaf
salt
freshly ground black pepper
600 ml (1 pint) brown stock
*Flaky pastry:*
175 g (6 oz) self-raising flour
⅓ teaspoon salt
100 g (4 oz) butter or margarine
1 teaspoon lemon juice
about 100 ml (3½ fl oz) iced water
1 small egg, beaten

*Preparation time: 55 minutes, plus cooling*
*Cooking time: 2¼-2¾ hours*
*Oven: 150°C, 300°F, Gas Mark 2;*
*then: 200°C, 400°F, Gas Mark 6;*
*then: 150°C, 300°F, Gas Mark 2*

1. Melt the butter in a frying pan, add the onion and cook until softened. Add the game and brown on all sides. Remove from the pan and reserve.
2. Add the steak and brown lightly.
3. Spread the steak on the bottom of a large pie dish and arrange the joints on top. Sprinkle the onion, bacon, mushrooms and herbs on top. Season to taste. Just cover with stock, cover with foil and simmer in a preheated oven until tender, about 1½-2 hours.
4. Meanwhile make the pastry. Sieve the flour and salt into a bowl. Rub into it 25 g (1 oz) of the fat and add the lemon juice. Add the water slowly, stirring all the time until a smooth paste is formed.
5. Roll out the dough lightly on a floured board, then dab it with small pieces of butter using a knife blade. Sprinkle with a pinch of flour. Fold the pastry towards you and pinch the edges, so that it forms an envelope. Roll as before, rolling away from the joined edge and towards the fold, so that the air is not forced out. Dab with butter again, sprinkle with flour, fold towards you and roll once more. Repeat until all the butter has been used and you have an oblong shape about 1 cm (½ inch) thick. Rest in the refrigerator.
6. Remove the dish from the oven and allow to cool. Heat the oven to the higher temperature. Add a little more stock to bring the liquid to 1 cm (½ inch) from the top of the meat.
7. Roll out the pastry and cut out a lid to fit the dish.

Cut a strip 2.5 cm (1 inch) wide and lay on the rim of the dish. Moisten with water, then lay on the pastry lid, pressing it down firmly. Knock back the edges and mark with a knife in ridges. Brush with beaten egg. Roll out the trimmings and use to make leaves or other decorations. Place on the lid and brush with egg again. Bake in a preheated oven 20 minutes.

8. Reduce the oven heat, place the pie lower in the oven and bake for a further 15-20 minutes.

# ROAST VENISON

*Serves 8*

1.75 kg (4 lb) joint of venison
50 g (2 oz) butter
*Marinade:*
2 medium onions, peeled and chopped
300 ml (½ pint) red wine
2 tablespoons red wine vinegar
4 tablespoons olive oil
2 bay leaves
1 teaspoon ground ginger
1 tablespoon brown sugar
2 teaspoons made mustard
salt
freshly ground black pepper

*Preparation time: 10 minutes, plus overnight marinating*
*Cooking time: approx. 3 hours 20 minutes*
*Oven: 160-180°C, 325-350°F, Gas Mark 3-4*

Allow the venison to hang for 2 days if it is very fresh.

1. Mix together all the marinade ingredients and pour into a casserole. Place the joint of venison in the marinade and leave for 24 hours. Turn the meat over several times during this period, so it absorbs the flavour of the mixture.
2. Lift the venison from the marinade and drain well, put into a roasting pan and spread with the butter. As venison is a dry meat it is a good idea to use a roasting bag, covered roasting pan or to wrap the meat in foil.
3. Roast the venison in a preheated oven allowing 40 minutes per 450 g (1 lb) and 40 minutes over.

LEFT: *Game pie; Roast venison illustrated on page 28*

# POACHER'S POT

*Serves 10-12*

1 rabbit or 1.25 kg (2¾ lb) chicken, jointed
2 pigeons, halved
2 old grouse or pheasants or 1 of each, jointed
50 g (2 oz) flour
2 medium turnips,
peeled and cut in 2.5 cm (1 inch) cubes
2 large onions, peeled and sliced
3 large carrots, scraped and cut in rings
1 kg (2 lb) cut of venison or 1 kg (2 lb) gammon joint
4 sprigs fresh thyme
4 sprigs fresh sage
4 sprigs fresh parsley
15 g (½ oz) salt
1 teaspoon freshly ground black pepper
1 large Savoy cabbage, outer leaves and hard stalk removed, quartered
300 ml (½ pint) red wine

*Preparation time: 1 hour*
*Cooking time: 2½ hours*

1. Place the rabbit and game joints in a bowl, and rub over with flour.
2. Put all the vegetables, except the cabbage, in a very large pot or preserving pan and place the game and rabbit joints on top of them. Next add the venison or gammon in one piece.
3. Sprinkle over the herbs, salt (if gammon is used, reduce the salt to ¼ oz) and black pepper. Add just enough water to cover all the meat.
4. Cover closely with a double layer of foil, bring to the boil, then simmer very slowly for 2½ hours. Stir from time to time, in case the vegetables stick to the bottom of the pan.
5. After 2 hours, add the cabbage and the red wine. Make sure at this point that the stock is gently boiling and taste for seasoning.
6. After another half hour lift out the venison or gammon, and carve it into thick slices. Cut the slices in half and put these back into the stew to warm through.
7. To serve, carefully ladle some stew into large soup plates or bowls standing on meat plates, making sure that each one has a large portion of cabbage, a joint or two of the game and some meat, as well as some root vegetables and plenty of gravy. Serve with crusty home-made bread or scones, to mop up the gravy.

# Quail Casserole

1.25 litres (2¼ pints) water
225 g (8 oz) bacon, rinded and cut into strips
75 g (3 oz) butter
8 quail, about 100 g (4 oz) each
475 ml (16 fl oz) chicken stock
250 ml (8 fl oz) Madeira
salt
freshly ground black pepper
275 g (10 oz) button mushrooms,
cleaned and quartered
15 g (½ oz) porcini mushrooms, reconstituted for 30
minutes in 250 ml (8 fl oz) warm water, then
drained well and chopped
3 tablespoons cornflour
120 ml (4 fl oz) double or whipping cream

*Preparation time: 20 minutes, plus 30 minutes reconstitution*
*Cooking time: 1¾ hours*

Though game is traditionally eaten 'high' or hung
for a period of time, quail must be eaten fresh. High
quail can have a powerful smell that is not particularly appetizing.

1. Bring the water to the boil in a medium saucepan.
   Add the bacon and cook for 1-2 minutes. Remove
   the pan from the heat, drain the bacon in a colander and set aside.
2. Melt 50 g (2 oz) of the butter in a flameproof casserole over a medium-low heat. Add the bacon
   and, stirring occasionally, cook for 10 minutes.
   Add the quail to the casserole and brown on all
   sides, turning the quail frequently. Drain off the
   excess fat and discard. Blend in the stock, 120 ml
   (4 fl oz) of the Madeira, salt and pepper. Cover the
   casserole. Cook over a medium-low heat for 30
   minutes.
3. While the quail are cooking, melt the remaining
   butter in a large frying pan over a medium heat.
   Add the button and reconstituted porcini mushrooms. Cover and cook for 10 minutes, shaking
   the pan frequently. Remove from the heat and set
   aside.
4. When the quail have cooked for 30 minutes, add
   the mushrooms to the casserole. Cover and continue cooking for another 20 minutes. A
5. Transfer the quail to a heated serving platter and
   keep warm. Increase the heat under the casserole
   to high. Combine the cornflour and remaining
   Madeira in a cup until smooth. Using a whisk, stir

into the casserole. Add the cream and let the mixture come to the boil. Boil for 2-3 minutes. Taste
and adjust the seasoning, if necessary, then
remove the sauce from the heat. Pour over the
quail and serve.

A The casserole can be made several hours in advance, covered and kept chilled. Simmer for 15 minutes before proceeding with the recipe.

# Pheasant and Port Casserole

*Serves 6*

*Marinade:*
450 ml (¾ pint) port
1 large onion, peeled and sliced
1 large carrot, peeled and thinly sliced
2 sticks celery, chopped
1 garlic clove, peeled and finely chopped
1 tablespoon fresh thyme leaves
or ½ teaspoon dried thyme
4 juniper berries, crushed
1 bay leaf, crumbled
salt
freshly ground black pepper
2 pheasants, about 1¼ kg (2½ lb) each, cleaned,
skinned and jointed
*To finish:*
75 g (3 oz) butter
15 g (½ oz) dried porcini mushrooms, reconstituted
in 250 ml (8 fl oz) warm water for 30 minutes, then
drained well and chopped
225 g (8 oz) field mushrooms, cleaned and sliced
25 g (1 oz) plain flour
300 ml (½ pint) pheasant or chicken stock
150 ml (¼ pint) double cream
1 tablespoon finely chopped fresh parsley,
to garnish

*Preparation time: 25 minutes,*
*plus overnight marinating and reconstituting*
*Cooking time: 1½ hours*
*Oven: 180°C, 350°F, Gas Mark 4*

1. Combine the port, onion, carrot, celery, garlic,
   thyme, juniper berries, bay leaf, salt and pepper in
   a deep bowl. Add the pheasant pieces and coat
   them evenly with the marinade. Cover and chill
   overnight. A

40

FROM THE LEFT: *Quail casserole; Pheasant and port casserole*

2. Remove the pheasant pieces from the marinade and pat dry with paper towels. Strain and reserve the marinade.

3. Heat 50 g (2 oz) of the butter in a large frying pan over a medium-high heat. Brown the pheasant pieces in the butter, turning occasionally, for 10 minutes. Transfer the pieces with a slotted spoon or tongs to a flameproof casserole. Set aside.

4. Melt the remaining butter in the frying pan over a medium heat. Add the porcini and field mushrooms. Cook, stirring occasionally, for 5 minutes. Blend in the flour and, stirring continuously, cook for 2-3 minutes. Lower the heat. Using a whisk, gradually add the stock and reserved marinade. Cook, whisking continuously, until the sauce comes to the boil and has slightly thickened. Remove the sauce from the heat and pour over the pheasant. Cover and cook in a preheated oven for 1 hour. A

5. Remove the casserole from the oven. Transfer the pheasant pieces with a slotted spoon or tongs to a heated serving dish. Keep warm in the oven while making the sauce.

6. Pour the sauce into a medium saucepan. Bring to the boil over a high heat. Add the cream and simmer for 2-3 minutes. Remove the sauce from the heat and pour over the pheasant pieces.

7. To serve, garnish the pheasant with the parsley. Crisp potato pancakes and steamed broccoli would go well with this dish.

A The pheasants may be marinated for up to 3 days, turning the pieces over daily. The casserole may be cooked earlier in the day, then covered and chilled. Reheat in a 180°C, 350°F, Gas Mark 4 oven for 30 minutes or until heated through, before proceeding with the recipe.

# JUGGED HARE

*Serves 6*

100 g (4 oz) fine oatmeal
salt
freshly ground white pepper
1 hare, cleaned, skinned and jointed
75 g (3 oz) butter
1 medium onion, peeled and stuck with cloves
1 large cooking apple, peeled, cored and sliced
1 small lemon, sliced
225 g (8 oz) mushrooms, cleaned and sliced
1 sprig each fresh thyme, parsley, marjoram, tied in
a bunch or 1 bouquet garni
3 bay leaves
120 ml (4 fl oz) red wine
600 ml (1 pint) beef stock
*Forcemeat balls:*
175 g (6 oz) breadcrumbs
50 g (2 oz) shredded suet
50 g (2 oz) bacon, finely chopped and fried crisp
2 teaspoons finely chopped fresh parsley
2 teaspoons dried herbs or 4 teaspoons finely
chopped fresh marjoram, thyme and sage
salt
freshly ground black pepper
1 egg, beaten well
40 g (1½ oz) butter

*Preparation time: 45 minutes*
*Cooking time: 3 hours*
*Oven: 180°C, 350°F, Gas Mark 4*

1. Season half the oatmeal with ½ teaspoon salt and ½ teaspoon pepper and rub it over the hare joints. Heat 50 g (2 oz) of the butter in a large frying pan, add the hare and fry quickly, turning, to seal and brown on all sides. Remove from the heat.
2. Place the head, neck and ribs of the hare (which will not be served, as there is little meat on them, but which will enrich the gravy) in the bottom of a large casserole. Sprinkle with half the remaining oatmeal.
3. Pack in the hare joints, then the onion, apple, lemon, mushrooms and herbs. Sprinkle with the remaining oatmeal and season. Combine the wine and stock and pour into the casserole.
4. Cover tightly and stand in a roasting tin. Pour in boiling water to come halfway up the sides of the casserole and cook in a preheated oven for 3 hours.
5. Mix together the breadcrumbs and the suet in a bowl. Add the bacon, parsley, herbs, salt and pepper. Stir the beaten egg into the mixture. Form into little balls about 2.5 cm (1 inch) in diameter.
6. Towards the end of the cooking time fry the forcemeat balls in the remaining butter.

7. Transfer the hare joints to a serving dish and strain the gravy, discarding the head, neck and ribs. Taste and adjust the seasoning, if necessary. Pour the gravy over the hare. Arrange the force-meat balls around the edge of the dish and serve very hot.

# PIGEONS IN PASTRY

*Serves 6*

750 g (1½ lb) Flaky pastry (page 38)
100 g (4 oz) butter
6 young pigeons, cleaned and trussed
100 g (4 oz) mushrooms, cleaned and sliced
1 teaspoon chopped fresh thyme or ½ teaspoon dried thyme
salt
freshly ground black pepper
3 tablespoons red wine or 2 tablespoons sherry
600 ml (1 pint) well-seasoned,
thickened brown gravy
1 egg, well beaten

*Preparation time: 30 minutes*
*Cooking time: 55 minutes*
*Oven: 230°C, 450°F, Gas Mark 8;*
*then: 180°C, 350°F, Gas Mark 4*

1. Roll out the pastry to about 5 mm (¼ inch) thickness and leave to rest in a cool place.
2. Heat the butter in a large frying pan, add the pigeons and fry, turning, to brown on all sides. Remove from the pan and set aside while lightly frying the mushrooms in the same butter.
3. Roll the pastry out again, a little thinner than before, and cut out 6 circles, each large enough to cover a pigeon completely.
4. Place a pigeon in the centre of each pastry circle, top with a few mushroom slices and sprinkle with the thyme, salt and pepper. Mix the wine with the gravy and pour a spoonful over each pigeon.
5. Lift the pastry up round each pigeon and pinch well together at the top to seal. Brush all over with the beaten egg.
6. Bake near the top of a preheated oven for 10 minutes, then move the pigeon parcels to the lower part of the oven, place a sheet of foil lightly over them and reduce the heat. Bake for a further 35 minutes. Meanwhile reheat the remaining gravy.
7. Transfer the pigeon parcels very carefully to a heated flat serving dish and serve immediately, with the gravy handed separately in a jug.

FROM THE BOTTOM: *Pigeons in pastry with gravy; Jugged hare*

# CHAPTER THREE

# FARMHOUSE FARE

Poultry, lamb, veal, pork and beef feature in these
recipes. They provide the main course for a Saturday
dinner, Sunday lunch or any other set meal when
everyone sits down round the dining table with plenty
of time to enjoy a spread of good food, well cooked.
The meats are tenderly roasted, braised, boiled or
pan-fried and served with delicious sauces to provide
the central attraction of the feast.

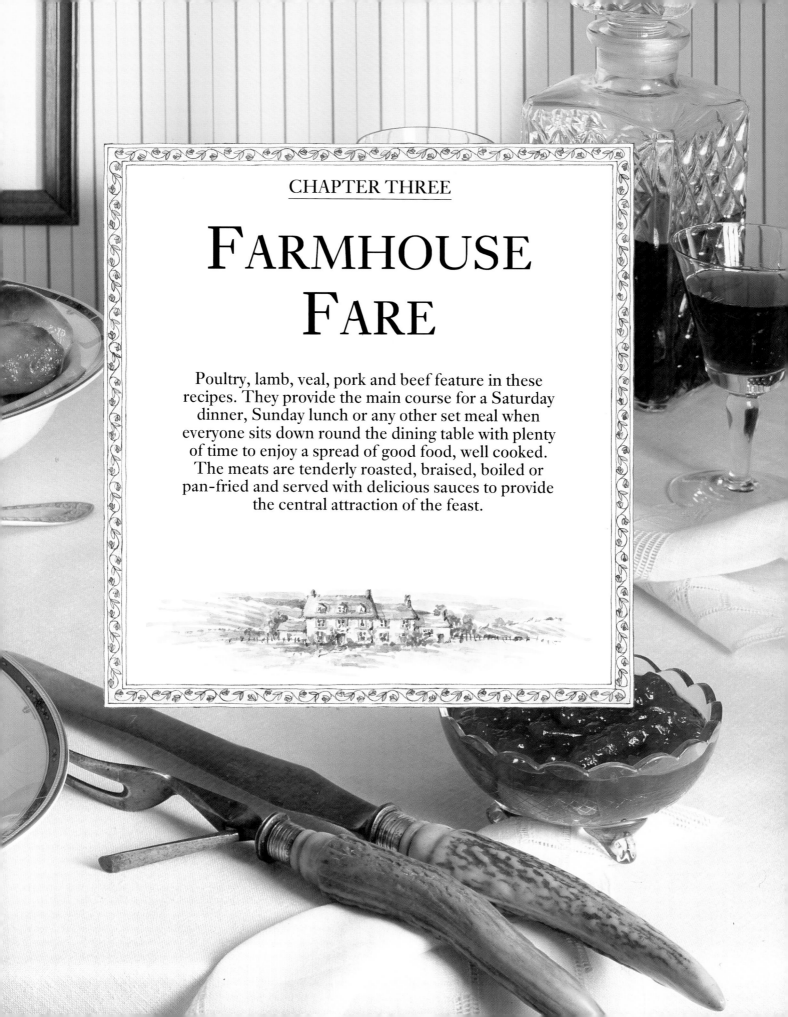

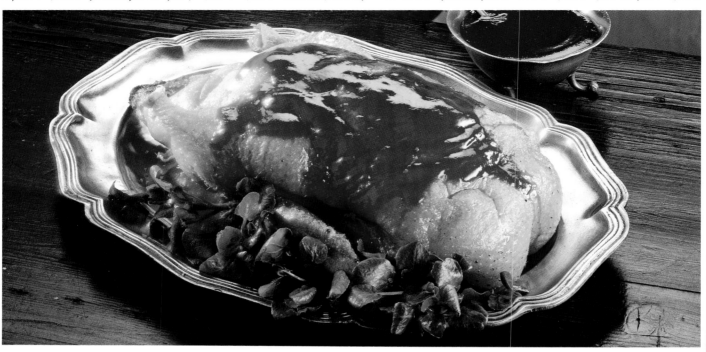

*Derwentwater duckling with Cumberland sauce*

# DERWENTWATER DUCKLING WITH CUMBERLAND SAUCE

Cumberland sauce can also be served cold with cold duck, chicken, pork and ham. It is worth making in quantity as it keeps well.

1.8 kg (4 lb) oven-ready duckling
salt
freshly ground black pepper
3 small onions, stuck with 2 cloves each
1 tablespoon butter or oil
2 tablespoons brandy
2 teaspoons cornflour
150 ml (¼ pint) stock (preferably made with the giblets)
*Cumberland sauce:*
225 g (8 oz) redcurrant jelly
6 tablespoons port
grated rind of 1 lemon
1 tablespoon orange juice
½ teaspoon made English mustard
watercress sprigs, to garnish

*Preparation time: 30 minutes*
*Cooking time: 1¾ hours*
*Oven: 200°C, 400°F, Gas Mark 6*

1. Wipe the duckling all over and sprinkle inside and out with salt and pepper.
2. Put the onions inside the body, then rub the breast and legs with the butter or oil.
3. Roast in a preheated oven for 1½ hours, basting as the fat comes out of the bird. If a lot of fat is released, pour some of it off during cooking. At the end of the cooking time, test that the duckling is ready by piercing the thigh with a skewer. The juices should run clear.
4. Meanwhile, make the Cumberland sauce: bring the redcurrant jelly and the port to the boil, reduce the heat and simmer until it is reduced by a quarter.
5. Remove from the heat and add the other ingredients, mix well and bring back to the boil for 2-3 minutes. Set aside.
6. Pour off the excess fat from the roasting pan, leaving only the juices. With the duckling still in the pan, place over a low heat. Warm the brandy in a ladle, pour over and set alight. When the flames die down, transfer the duckling to a warmed serving dish and keep warm.
7. Cream the cornflour with a little of the stock, add to the pan juices over a low flame and keep stirring until it is all quite smooth.
8. Add the Cumberland sauce, mixing well and scraping down the sides of the pan. Pour a little over the duck and serve the rest separately.
9. Serve garnished with watercress.

# HINDLE WAKES CHICKEN

Hindle Wakes chicken has come down through the ages almost unchanged. The Wake was originally the feast on the eve of the dedication of a church, which subsequently degenerated into a fair with much carousing. The white meat with its black filling and yellow and green garnish looks very medieval.

*Serves 4-6*

1 chicken, about 2 kg (4½ lb)
1 large onion, sliced
150 ml (¼ pint) vinegar
1 tablespoon brown sugar
*Stuffing:*
100 g (4 oz) fresh breadcrumbs
225 g (8 oz) prunes, soaked, stoned and chopped
salt
freshly ground black pepper
pinch of ground cinnamon
pinch of ground mace
2 teaspoons dried mixed herbs
1 tablespoon shredded suet or melted butter
2 tablespoons lemon juice
*Sauce:*
25 g (1 oz) butter
25 g (1 oz) flour
450 ml (¾ pint) chicken stock
1 tablespoon lemon juice

*To garnish:*
finely grated peel of 2 lemons
12 prunes, stoned
1 lemon, thinly sliced
parsley sprigs
1 tablespoon chopped parsley

*Preparation time: 45 minutes*
*Cooking time: 3½ hours, plus cooling*

1. Mix together all the stuffing ingredients very well, then stuff the chicken cavity with this mixture, securing it firmly.
2. Put the stuffed bird into a large saucepan with the sliced onion, seasoning to taste. Barely cover with cold water.
3. Add the vinegar and sugar. Bring to the boil, then lower the heat, cover, and simmer very slowly for about 2½-3 hours. Allow to cool in the broth and skim the top when it is quite cold.
4. When needed, lift the chicken carefully from the saucepan, straining it well, and put on to a large dish. Reserve the stock. Remove all the skin from the bird.
5. To make the sauce, melt the butter in a small saucepan, add the flour and cook for 1 minute.
8. Cover the bird with the lemon sauce and sprinkle the lemon peel all over. Leave in a cold place, but not necessarily the refrigerator.
9. Garnish with the prunes, lemon slices and parsley sprigs, and sprinkle with chopped parsley.

*Hindle Wakes chicken*

# HONEY ROASTED TURKEY WITH CANDIED POTATOES

This way of cooking turkeys, which is unsurpassed, comes from Norfolk. The potatoes will be deliciously candied from the honey, while taking up the flavour of the turkey from the juice. Gravy should be made separately, from the giblets, as the honey in the pan makes it too sweet.

*Serves 8-10*
225 g (8 oz) medium thick honey
100 g (4 oz) butter
3.5-5.5 kg (8-12 lb) oven-ready turkey
1.4 kg (3 lb) potatoes, peeled and halved

*Allow 15 minutes roasting per 450 g (1 lb)*
*Preparation time: 5 minutes, plus standing*
*Oven: 200°C, 400°F, Gas Mark 6;*
*then: 180°C, 350°F, Gas Mark 4*

1. Melt the honey and butter together and stir well. Place the turkey in a roasting tin and pour the mixture all over it. Allow to stand for an hour or so, basting occasionally with the mixture which has run off into the tray.
2. Arrange the potatoes around the turkey and roast in a preheated oven for 40 minutes. The honey will make an almost black crust over the bird, sealing in the flavour. Baste with the mixture that has run off and reduce the oven heat.
3. Return to the oven for a further 30 minutes, then baste again. Cover the turkey with foil and continue cooking.
4. 15 minutes before serving, remove the foil so that the skin may crisp.

*Honey roasted turkey with candied potatoes*

# ROAST GOOSE

*Serves 6-8*

1 oven-ready goose, about 3-4 kg (7-9 lb)
25 g (1 oz) butter or margarine
1 onion, peeled and finely chopped
goose livers, finely chopped
2 teaspoons dried sage
1-2 tablespoons chopped fresh parsley
salt
freshly ground black pepper
75 g (3 oz) fresh white breadcrumbs
1 egg, beaten
300 ml (½ pint) dry white wine
300 ml (½ pint) stock made with the goose giblets
(or chicken stock)
2 teaspoons cornflour
little lemon juice (optional)
*To garnish:*
button onions
carrot sticks
parsley sprigs

*Preparation time: 30 minutes*
*Cooking time: 2-2¾ hours*
*Oven: 220°C, 426°F, Gas Mark 7;*
*then: 180°C, 350°F, Gas Mark 4*

1. If using a frozen goose make sure it is completely thawed – allow at least 24 hours at room temperature. Remove the giblets and any excess fat inside the cavity.
2. For the stuffing, melt the butter in a frying pan and fry the onion until soft. Add the livers and cook for a few minutes, stirring frequently until cooked through. Turn the mixture into a bowl, add the sage, parsley, salt and pepper, then the breadcrumbs. Add sufficient beaten egg to give a softish stuffing.
3. Use this stuffing to stuff the neck end of the goose and fasten with a skewer. Truss the bird lightly and prick all over with a fork or large darning needle.
4. Place the goose in a roasting tin, on a wire tray. Combine the wine and stock and pour over the goose.
5. Roast in a preheated oven for 20 minutes, then remove from the oven. Baste with the pan juices, then cover the goose with greaseproof paper. Reduce the temperature to moderate, then return the goose to the oven and roast, allowing 15 min-

utes per 450 g (1 lb). Baste again halfway through the cooking time and remove the paper for the last 20 minutes to allow the skin to brown.
6. Place the goose on a warmed serving dish and keep warm. Spoon off all the grease from the pan juices, using paper towels to mop it all up. Strain the juices into a pan, add the cornflour blended with a little cold water and stir over a medium heat until the sauce thickens.
7. Garnish the goose with lightly-cooked onions and carrots and the sprigs of parsley.

# ALMOND-COATED TURKEY

4 slices breast of turkey,
about 100-125 g (4-5 oz each)
50 g (2 oz) chopped, blanched almonds
25 g (1 oz) soft margarine
1 tablespoon sunflower oil
2 teaspoons wholewheat flour
150 ml (¼ pint) plain unsweetened yogurt
2 tablespoons chicken stock
1 tablespoon grated orange rind
4 tablespoons orange juice
salt
freshly ground black pepper
pinch of ground cinnamon
2 oranges, peeled and segmented, to garnish

*Preparation time: 15 minutes*
*Cooking time: 15 minutes*

1. Coat the turkey in the chopped almonds, pressing the nuts well into the meat.
2. Heat the margarine and oil in a frying pan and fry the turkey slices over a moderate heat for 5 minutes on each side. Remove them from the pan and keep them warm.
3. In a small pan, stir the flour to a paste with a little of the yogurt, then pour on the remainder and bring to the boil, stirring. Simmer for 3 minutes.
4. Stir the stock, orange rind and juice into the frying pan and bring to the boil. Pour on the yogurt, season with salt, pepper and cinnamon and simmer for 1 minute.
5. Pour the sauce on to a heated serving dish. Place the turkey slices on the sauce and garnish with the orange segments.

# LOIN OF LAMB STUFFED WITH CUCUMBER AND MINT

2 shallots, peeled and chopped
15 g (½ oz) butter
100 g (4 oz) cucumber, peeled and grated
1 tablespoon chopped fresh mint
50 g (2 oz) fresh white breadcrumbs
1 egg yolk
salt
freshly ground black pepper
1 boned loin of lamb, 1 kg (2 lb) boned weight

*Preparation time: 20 minutes, plus cooling*
*Cooking time: 1½ hours*
*Oven: 180°C, 350°F, Gas Mark 4*

1. Fry the shallots in the butter until soft, add the cucumber, mint, breadcrumbs, egg yolk, salt and pepper. Mix well, then leave to cool.
2. Lay the lamb out and score the fat in a diamond pattern. Turn over and spread the stuffing over the meat. Roll up and tie with string.
3. Cook in a preheated oven for about 1½ hours. Remove the string before serving with the Sauce paloise (see right) handed separately.
4. Serve with new potatoes and broad beans.

*Loin of lamb stuffed with cucumber and mint; Sauce paloise*

# SAUCE PALOISE

4 tablespoons wine vinegar
2 tablespoons water
1 teaspoon dried mint
6 black peppercorns
1 shallot, peeled and chopped
2 egg yolks
75 g (3 oz) unsalted butter
1 tablespoon chopped fresh mint
salt

*Preparation time: 10 minutes*
*Cooking time: 10 minutes*

This is a variation of the classic Béarnaise sauce with mint used instead of tarragon, thus echoing the flavour of the lamb stuffing.

1. Put the vinegar, water, dried mint, peppercorns and shallot into a pan. Boil until reduced to 2 tablespoons. Strain well.
2. Put the egg yolks in the top of a double saucepan or in a bowl over a pan of simmering water and whisk in the vinegar mixture until the mixture is light and fluffy. Take care that the water underneath does not boil.
3. Add the butter, a little at a time, whisking well. Stir in the fresh mint. Add salt to taste. Serve the sauce warm with the loin of lamb.

# CHICKEN IN A BRICK

*Serves 4-6*

1.5 kg (3¼ lb) oven-ready chicken
1 tablespoon lemon juice
*Filling:*
25 g (1 oz) soft margarine
1 small onion, peeled and finely chopped
1 celery stick, finely chopped
100 g (4 oz) dried pears, chopped
50 g (2 oz) fresh wholewheat breadcrumbs
50 g (2 oz) Brazil nuts, chopped
1 teaspoon grated lemon rind
salt
freshly ground black pepper
1 small egg, beaten
parsley sprigs, to garnish

*Preparation time: 35 minutes, plus soaking*
*Cooking time: 1 hour 50 minutes*
*Oven: 220°C, 425°F, Gas Mark 7 (do not preheat)*

Although a chicken brick is used in this recipe, you can, of course, cook the chicken with dried pear stuffing in a roasting pan in the oven in the normal way.

1. Soak the chicken brick in warm water for 15 minutes. To make the filling, melt the margarine and fry the onion and celery together over moderate heat for 3 minutes, stirring once or twice. Remove from the heat and stir in the pears, breadcrumbs, Brazil nuts and lemon rind and season with salt and pepper. Beat in the egg. F
2. Wipe the chicken inside and out with a damp cloth. Spoon the filling into the cavity and tie the legs together with string. Sprinkle the lemon juice over the bird.
3. Line the chicken brick with greaseproof paper. Place the bird in the brick, cover with greaseproof paper and put on the lid.
4. Place the chicken brick in a cold oven and set the heat as indicated. Cook for 1¾ hours, or until the chicken is cooked. To test, pierce the thickest part of the thigh with a fine skewer: the juices should run clear.
5. Transfer the chicken to a heated serving dish and garnish with parsley sprigs. Pour off the juices from the brick and serve separately.

F Freeze the filling for up to 1 month. Thaw completely before using.

# DUCK WITH BLACKCURRANT SAUCE

1 oven-ready duck 1.5 kg (3½ lb), halved
salt
freshly ground black pepper
1 tablespoon chopped fresh rosemary
4 tablespoons brandy
olive oil
*Sauce:*
25 g (1 oz) butter
1 small onion, peeled and finely chopped
1 × 300 g (11 oz) can blackcurrants in syrup
2 tablespoons red wine vinegar
fresh rosemary, to garnish

*Preparation time: 20 minutes, plus marinating*
*Cooking time: 1 hour 10 minutes*
*Oven: 200°C, 400°F, Gas Mark 6*

1. Put the halved duck into a large shallow dish. Pierce in a few places with a fine skewer. Add salt and pepper to taste, the rosemary, brandy and a sprinkling of olive oil. Cover and marinate in the refrigerator for at least 6 hours or overnight.
2. Remove the duck, reserving any marinade. Place the duck halves on a rack in a roasting tin, skin side uppermost. Rub a little olive oil into the duck skin. Roast in a preheated oven for 1 hour or until the duck is tender.
3. Meanwhile, prepare the sauce. Melt the butter in a saucepan, add the onion and fry gently for 3 minutes. Add the blackcurrants, syrup, wine vinegar and reserved duck marinade. Bring to the boil and simmer gently for 5 minutes.
4. Purée the sauce in a blender or food processor until smooth. Return to the saucepan and heat through. Taste and adjust the seasoning.
5. Place the duck halves on a serving dish, spoon the sauce over the top and garnish with rosemary.

# Braised stuffed shoulder of lamb

*Serves 6*

*Stuffing:*
50 g (2 oz) butter
1 small onion, peeled and finely chopped
75 g (3 oz) mushrooms, cleaned and sliced
100 g (4 oz) crustless day-old white bread, diced
75 g (3 oz) pine nuts
25 g (1 oz) chopped fresh parsley
2 sticks celery, finely chopped
2 eggs, beaten
1 tablespoon chopped fresh tarragon or
1 teaspoon dried tarragon
1 tablespoon chopped fresh mint or
1 teaspoon dried mint
½ teaspoon paprika
salt
freshly ground black pepper
*Lamb:*
2 garlic cloves, peeled and cut into slivers
1 × 1½ kg (3¾ lb) shoulder of lamb, boned,
pocket cut and the bones reserved
1 tablespoon rosemary leaves or
½ teaspoon dried rosemary
salt
freshly ground black pepper
3 tablespoons vegetable oil
500 ml (18 fl oz) lamb or beef stock
50 g (2 oz) onion, peeled and diced
50 g (2 oz) carrots, peeled and diced
25 g (1 oz) celery, diced
150 g (5 oz) potatoes, peeled and diced
2 tablespoons cornflour
50 ml (2 fl oz) port
4 sprigs fresh mint, to garnish

*Preparation time: 45 minutes*
*Cooking time: 2½ hours*
*Oven: 160°C, 325°F, Gas Mark 3*

The amount of bread needed for this stuffing may have to be altered, depending on the bread you use. A simple way of determining if you have the correct amount of diced bread is to put it into a pint measuring jug: if you have just over a pint, you will have enough to make the required amount of stuffing.

The lamb shoulder must be boned. When it is boned, you will find that there is a 'pocket' in the centre of the shoulder. Cut the pocket to extend it almost, but not through, the shoulder. One end of the shoulder should still be intact. The stuffing will then be placed in the pocket.

1. For the stuffing, melt the butter in a large frying pan over a medium heat. Add the onion and mushrooms and cook for 10 minutes, stirring frequently. Remove the mixture from the heat and tip into a large glass or ceramic bowl.
2. Add the remaining ingredients for the stuffing, then stir gently until well combined. Set aside.
3. Insert the slivers of garlic under the skin of the lamb. Lay the lamb out flat, skin side down, on a working surface. Place the stuffing evenly in the pocket of the shoulder. Close the open end of the shoulder with 4 metal skewers. Roll the meat to tuck the long ends of the roast underneath, then tie firmly with string. Sprinkle the roast with the rosemary, salt and pepper.
4. Heat the oil in a large frying pan over a medium heat. Place the roast in the frying pan. Brown on all sides, using 2 large spoons to turn the roast. Remove the roast from the pan and set aside.
5. Pour 250 ml (8 fl oz) of the stock into a large casserole. Add the roast and the reserved bones. Cover and place in a preheated oven. Cook for 45 minutes.
6. Remove the casserole from the oven, then add all but 50 ml (2 fl oz) of the remaining stock, the onions, carrots, celery and potatoes. Cover and return to the oven. Cook for 1 hour.
7. Remove the casserole from the oven. Transfer the roast to a heated platter and keep warm. Discard the bones from the sauce, then skim off the fat.
8. Bring the sauce to the boil in a large saucepan over a high heat. Thoroughly combine the cornflour, port and the rest of the stock in a large cup. Whisk into the sauce, then cook for 4-5 minutes, stirring constantly, until thick and smooth. Strain the sauce into a heated sauceboat.
9. To serve, place the roast on a heated serving platter and garnish with the mint. Serve the sauce separately. Serve with boiled new potatoes and a colourful vegetable, such as mange-tout or baby sweetcorn.

# LAMB SHREWSBURY

FROM THE LEFT: *Braised stuffed shoulder of lamb; Lamb Shrewsbury*

*Serves 6*

50 g (2 oz) plain flour
1 tablespoon finely chopped fresh rosemary
or ½ teaspoon dried rosemary
salt
freshly ground black pepper
6 × 175 g (6 oz) loin lamb chops
50 g (2 oz) butter
1 onion, peeled and finely chopped
1 carrot, peeled and sliced
1 large tomato, peeled, seeded and diced
1 garlic clove, peeled and finely chopped
2 tablespoons tomato purée
120 ml (4 fl oz) port
900 ml (1½ pints) beef stock
4 tablespoons redcurrant jelly
1 bunch watercress, to garnish

*Preparation time: 15 minutes*
*Cooking time: 1½ hours*
*Oven: 180°C, 350°F, Gas Mark 4*

1. Combine the flour, rosemary, salt and pepper and coat the chops in the mixture.
2. Heat the butter in a large flameproof casserole over a moderate heat. Add the chops and brown on one side for 5 minutes. Turn the chops over and continue to brown for 5 minutes.
3. Add the onion, carrot, tomato and garlic to the casserole. Blend in the tomato purée, port, stock and redcurrant jelly. Cover and place in a pre-heated oven. Cook for 1 hour. $\boxed{\text{A}}$
4. Remove the chops from the sauce and place on a heated serving platter. Strain the sauce and return to the cleaned casserole. Simmer for 10 minutes over a moderate heat until thick.
5. To serve, pour the sauce over the chops and garnish with the watercress.

$\boxed{\text{A}}$ The casserole may be made one day in advance, covered and kept chilled. Simmer for 10-20 minutes, until heated through.

# VEGETABLE-BRAISED VEAL ROAST

*Serves 8*

65 g (3 oz) butter
1 × 2¼ kg (5 lb) loin of veal, trimmed of fat, boned, tenderloin and kidneys replaced evenly inside the loin, rolled and tied
3 carrots, peeled and cut into julienne strips
3 leeks, white part only, cut into julienne strips
1 large tomato, peeled, seeded and diced
1 large garlic clove, peeled and finely chopped
½ tablespoon fresh thyme leaves or
½ teaspoon dried thyme
salt
freshly ground white pepper
475 ml (16 fl oz) veal or chicken stock
250 ml (8 fl oz) dry white wine
1½ tablespoons cornflour
50 ml (2 fl oz) dry sherry
4 sprigs watercress, to garnish

*Preparation time: 35-45 minutes*
*Cooking time: 2¾ hours*
*Oven: 180°C, 350°F, Gas Mark 4*

Ask the butcher to prepare the veal roast. The loin must be trimmed of most of its fat and boned. (Ask for the bones - they make a good stock.) The tenderloin and kidneys are then placed inside the loin where the bones used to be. Finally, the roast is rolled and tied with string.

1. Melt 50 g (2 oz) of the butter in a large flameproof casserole over a medium heat. Place the roast in the casserole, then brown on all sides, using 2 large spoons to turn the roast. Remove the roast from the casserole and set aside.
2. Add the carrots and leeks to the casserole. Cook, stirring frequently, for 2 minutes. Lower the heat, then add the tomato, garlic, thyme, salt and pepper. Cook gently for 2 minutes, stirring occasionally. Remove the casserole from the heat and set aside to cool for a few minutes.
3. Cut a piece of greaseproof paper 40 × 40 cm (16 × 16 inches). Lay the paper on a working surface, then coat with the remaining butter. Spread half of the vegetable mixture evenly on the paper. Place the roast in the centre of the vegetables. Coat the roast with the remaining vegetables.

Bring up the sides of the paper to enclose the roast, then fold the top securely. Fold the sides securely underneath the roast. Return the wrapped roast to the casserole. Pour the stock and wine over the roast and place the casserole on the stove. Bring to the boil over a medium heat, then cover. Transfer the casserole to a preheated oven, then cook for 2 hours, until the juices run clear when the roast is pricked with a skewer.

4. Remove the roast from the casserole and place on a heated platter. Place the casserole over a medium heat on the stove. Combine the cornflour and sherry in a cup until smooth. Whisk into the casserole, then bring the sauce to the boil, stirring constantly. Add salt and pepper to taste.
5. Unwrap the roast and cut the strings off. Add the vegetables and juices from the roast to the sauce. Return the sauce to the boil.
6. To serve, slice the roast and place on a heated serving platter. Coat the slices with the sauce, then garnish with the watercress.

# STUFFED VEAL ROLLS

*Stuffing:*
40 g (1½ oz) butter
450 g (1 lb) lean minced pork
1 small onion, peeled and finely chopped
1 celery stalk, finely chopped
75 g (3 oz) field mushrooms, cleaned and chopped
1 garlic clove, peeled and finely chopped
2 tablespoons finely chopped fresh parsley
salt
freshly ground black pepper
8 veal escalopes, about 50 g (2 oz) each and
15 cm (6 inches) wide
*Sauce:*
50 g (2 oz) butter
2 medium onions, peeled and thinly sliced
1 garlic clove, peeled and finely chopped
250 ml (8 fl oz) dry white wine
275 ml (9 fl oz) beef stock
2 teaspoons cornflour
1 tablespoon chopped fresh parsley, to garnish

*Preparation time: 30 minutes*
*Cooking time: 1¾ hours*
*Oven: 180°C, 350°F, Gas Mark 4*

1. To make the stuffing, melt 15 g (½ oz) of the butter in a large frying pan over a moderate heat. Add the

pork then, stirring frequently, cook for 10 minutes until browned. Remove the pork to a medium bowl with a slotted spoon and set aside.

2. Melt the remaining butter in the frying pan over a moderate heat. Add the onion, celery, mushrooms and garlic. Cook for 10 minutes, stirring frequently. Remove from the heat. Blend into the cooked pork. Stir in the parsley, salt and pepper, then set aside.

3. Lay the escalopes on a working surface. Place 2 tablespoons of the stuffing on one end of each escalope. Roll up to enclose the stuffing, then tie securely with string. A

4. Melt 25 g (1 oz) of the butter in a large flameproof casserole over a medium-high heat. Add the veal rolls and, turning frequently, cook for 5 minutes, until browned on all sides. Remove the casserole from the heat and set aside.

5. Melt the remaining butter in a large frying pan over a moderate heat. Add the onions and cook for 5 minutes, stirring frequently. Stir in the garlic and continue cooking for 1 minute. Remove from the heat and cover the veal rolls with the onion mixture.

6. Return the frying pan to a moderate heat. Add the wine and 250 ml (8 fl oz) of the beef stock. Cook for 2-3 minutes, stirring constantly. Add the salt and pepper. Remove the wine mixture from the heat and pour over the veal rolls. Cover and transfer the casserole to a preheated oven. Cook for 20-30 minutes.

7. Remove the casserole from the oven. Transfer the veal rolls with a slotted spoon to a working surface. Discard the strings. Arrange the rolls on a heated serving dish. Place the casserole dish over a medium-high heat. Combine the cornflour and remaining stock in a small bowl until smooth. Gradually pour the cornflour mixture in the casserole, stirring constantly. Bring to the boil and simmer until smooth and thick.

8. To serve, coat the veal rolls with the sauce and garnish with the parsley.

A The veal rolls may be prepared earlier in the day, covered and chilled.

TOP: *Vegetable-braised veal roast;*
BOTTOM: *Stuffed veal rolls*

FROM THE LEFT: *Fillets of pork; Salmi of duck*

# Fillets of pork

225 g (8 oz) large prunes, soaked for 3 hours,
stoned and finely chopped,
reserving the soaking liquid
75 g (3 oz) white breadcrumbs
1 tablespoon finely chopped onion,
softened in a little butter
2 fillets of pork, each about 350 g (12 oz),
trimmed and halved crossways
40 g (1½ oz) flour, plus 2 tablespoons seasoned flour
salt
freshly ground pepper
75 g (3 oz) butter
150 ml (¼ pint) good white stock
(a bouillon cube will do)
150 ml (¼ pint) double cream
1 tablespoon brandy

*Preparation time: 20 minutes, plus soaking*
*Cooking time: 55 minutes*
*Oven: 180°C, 350°F, Gas Mark 4*

1. Mix the prunes with the breadcrumbs and onion.
2. Split each fillet in half lengthways. Spread the lower halves with the prune filling, then replace the top halves, like long sandwiches. Tie securely at intervals with fine twine.
3. Rub the stuffed fillets with seasoned flour and place in a shallow ovenproof dish. Melt the butter and pour over. Bake, tightly covered, for 40 minutes in a preheated oven.
4. Remove the fillets from the oven and pour off the butter and juices into a small pan. Return the pork fillets to the oven, uncovered, to bake for a further 15 minutes, so that the tops are lightly browned. Remove the strings.

# Salmi of Duck

*Serves 4-6*

2 oven-ready ducks or 3 wild ducks, roasted for 30
minutes only and allowed to cool
1 medium onion, peeled and finely chopped
40 g (1½ oz) butter
1 tablespoon plain flour
1 teaspoon dried thyme
1 teaspoon dried parsley
2 bay leaves
¼ teaspoon grated nutmeg
grated rind of 1 orange
2 teaspoons redcurrant jelly
salt
freshly ground pepper
150 ml (¼ pint) red wine
1 tablespoon brandy
100 g (4 oz) mushrooms, cleaned,
sliced and lightly fried in butter
2 teaspoons lemon juice

*Preparation time: 45 minutes*
*Cooking time: 2½ hours*

1. Carve all the meat from the ducks, cutting the breast in long slices. Set aside in the refrigerator.
2. Put the bones in a saucepan, just cover with salted water and boil for at least 1½ hours. Strain off the stock.
3. Fry the onion in the butter until just transparent and golden. Stir in the flour, cook for a minute and gradually stir in the stock. Add the herbs, nutmeg and orange rind, then stir in the redcurrant jelly. Season with salt and pepper and simmer for 30 minutes, uncovered, stirring occasionally, until the sauce is as thick as double cream.
4. Strain the sauce through a sieve into another saucepan, add the wine, brandy and mushrooms and simmer for 5 or 6 minutes. Add the lemon juice.
5. Check the seasoning and add the pieces of duck. Leave on the lowest possible heat for another 15 minutes, so that the duck is heated through, but do not allow it to boil.
6. Pour into a serving dish and serve immediately.

*Variation:*
This recipe is equally good with pheasant or partridge.

5. To make the sauce, stir the flour into the butter and pork juices, then add the prune juice and the stock. Boil for 3 minutes.
6. Stir in the cream, then the brandy. Do not allow to boil again, but keep warm until the fillets are ready.
7. Pour the sauce round the pork and serve immediately.

*Variation:*
The cream and butter can be replaced by 150 ml (¼ pint) milk and 100 g (4 oz) margarine, for a plainer dish if preferred.

# Baked ulster ham

*Serves 8*

1.75 kg (4 lb) corner of gammon, soaked overnight
2 whole cloves
4 black peppercorns
1 teaspoon brown sugar
*Topping:*
25 g (1 oz) butter
50 g (2 oz) brown sugar
pinch of ground cinnamon
1 tablespoon Bushmill's whiskey
150 ml (¼ pint) Guinness

*Preparation time: 20 minutes, plus soaking overnight*
*Cooking time: 2 hours*
*Oven: 190°C, 375°F, Gas Mark 5*

1. Strain the soaked gammon and scrape the outer skin, then put into a large saucepan and barely cover with cold water, adding the cloves, peppercorns and sugar.
2. Bring to the boil, remove any scum, then reduce to a simmer. Cover and cook for 1½ hours.
3. Remove the gammon, cool slightly but do not let it get cold, and peel off the skin.
4. To make the topping, mix the butter, brown sugar, cinnamon and whiskey together well. Score the top of the gammon fat with a diamond pattern and press the topping on to it firmly.
5. Lift on to an ovenproof dish and pour the Guinness around.
6. Bake in a preheated oven for 30 minutes or until the topping is crisp and golden. Serve hot or cold.

# Stuffed pork steak

*Serves 6*

2 pork fillets, weighing about 1.4 kg (3 lb), trimmed
175 g (6 oz) fresh breadcrumbs
3 tablespoons milk
1 medium onion, peeled and finely chopped
1 teaspoon grated lemon rind
1 teaspoon lemon juice
pinch of ground nutmeg or mace
½ teaspoon dried sage
½ teaspoon dried thyme
1 tablespoon chopped fresh parsley
salt
freshly ground black pepper
50 g (2 oz) butter
300 ml (½ pint) beef stock

*Preparation time: 40 minutes*
*Cooking time: 1½ hours*
*Oven: 200°C, 400°F, Gas Mark 6;*
*then: 180°C, 350°F, Gas Mark 4*

1. Lay the pork fillets on a board and cut down the middle, not right through the meat, so you can pull the 2 sides apart. Gently spread them open and beat down with the blunt side of the knife so that they are almost flat. Score them lightly down the length, again not cutting right through, so that they have a flattish rectangular shape.
2. Make the stuffing by mixing together the breadcrumbs, milk, onion, lemon rind and juice, spice, herbs, salt and pepper, to form a thick paste.
3. Divide the stuffing between the 2 pork steaks and either fold them over sideways or roll up, in either case securing with a cocktail stick.
4. Rub all over with the butter, season lightly and put into a roasting pan. Add the stock, cover loosely with foil and put into a preheated oven for 20 minutes. Reduce the temperature and cook for 1 hour.
5. Baste once or twice and turn each pork steak if necessary. Take off the foil 10 minutes from the end and brown the tops a little.
6. To make the gravy, transfer the meat to a serving dish and keep warm. Boil up the liquid in the roasting pan, reduce and season to taste.

# BRAISED HAM

1 kg (2¼ lb) forelock or middle gammon
300 ml (½ pint) pale ale
freshly ground black pepper
2 tablespoons honey
4 tablespoons demerara sugar
1 teaspoon dry mustard
12 cloves
*To garnish:*
orange wedges
watercress

*Preparation time: 15 minutes, plus soaking*
*Cooking time: 1 hour 10 minutes*
*Oven: 180°C, 350°F, Gas Mark 4;*
*then: 200°C, 400°F, Gas Mark 6*

1. Soak the ham in cold water to cover for several hours. Drain, discarding the water.
2. Place the ham in a casserole with the pale ale, sprinkle with pepper and cook, covered, in a preheated oven for 40 minutes.
3. Remove the ham from the casserole and discard half the ale. Cut away the skin from the ham and score the fat diagonally.
4. Rub a mixture of the honey, sugar and dry mustard over the ham. Stud cloves into the ham surface in a diamond pattern and return the remaining ham and ale to the casserole.
5. Cook, uncovered, at the higher temperature for a further 30 minutes, basting the joint every 10 minutes. Serve the ham garnished with wedges of orange and watercress.

FROM THE LEFT: *Baked Ulster ham; Stuffed pork steak*

## POT ROASTED BEEF

4 tablespoons vegetable oil
25 g (1 oz) butter
1.25-1.5 kg (2½-3 lb) topside or silverside of beef
2 large onions, peeled and quartered
2 large carrots, scraped and cut into
1 cm (½ inch) slices
1 bouquet garni or 2 sprigs each fresh thyme,
parsley and marjoram
4 black peppercorns
½ teaspoon salt
150 ml (¼ pint) red wine mixed with
450 ml (¾ pint) water
2 teaspoons cornflour

*Preparation time: 30 minutes*
*Cooking time: 3 hours 20 minutes*
*Oven: 150°C, 300°F, Gas Mark 2*

1. Heat the oil and butter in a flameproof casserole, add the beef and turn until browned.
2. Reduce the heat and pack the vegetables all round the beef. Add the herbs, peppercorns and salt. Pour in the wine and water.
3. Cover the casserole closely with foil and then its lid and cook in a preheated oven for 3 hours, until the beef is tender and cooked through.
4. Transfer the beef to a heated serving dish. Discard the herbs. Lift out the vegetables with a perforated spoon and place round the beef. Keep hot while making the sauce.
5. Bring the cooking liquid in the casserole to the boil. Mix the cornflour with a little water to make a smooth paste, pour a little of the boiling gravy on to it, stirring well, and pour back into the boiling gravy in the casserole, stirring constantly. If the sauce is too thick, thin with a little stock or water and return to the boil.
6. Pour the sauce over the beef and vegetables and serve with Brussels sprouts which have been boiled, then tossed with fried bacon, sprinkled with grated cheese and breadcrumbs and browned under the grill.

## CHRISTMAS COLD SPICED BEEF AND HOT SOUP

Skirt of beef, boned and rolled by the butcher, was traditionally used for this recipe, but topside or silverside, though more expensive, can be used without rolling if more convenient. With these there is, of course, no waste.

*Serves 6-8*

2.75 kg (6 lb) skirt of beef, boned and rolled, bones and trimmings reserved, or 1.75 kg (4 lb) topside or silverside, with extra beef bones
225 g (8 oz) salt
2 teaspoons freshly ground black pepper
1 teaspoon ground cloves
1 teaspoon dried thyme
1 teaspoon dried marjoram
1 teaspoon cayenne pepper
1 teaspoon paprika
450 g (1 lb) carrots, scraped and sliced
450 g (1 lb) onions, peeled and quartered
1 head celery, cut in 5 cm (2 inch) lengths
2-3 tablespoons whisky (optional)
*To garnish:*
225 g (8 oz) gherkins, finely sliced

*Preparation time: 45 minutes, plus salting and cooling*
*Cooking time: 3½ hours*

1. Lay the skirt of beef out flat, skin downward, and rub in most of the salt. If using topside or silverside, cut 3 slashes about 1 cm (½ inch) deep into the top and rub in salt in the same way. Leave the meat to stand in the refrigerator overnight.
2. The next day, drain off all the liquid and wipe the meat, removing any surface salt. Mix together all the herbs and spices and rub them into the meat, particularly into the slashes in the topside. Roll the skirt up tightly and tie with string in 3 or 4 places. (Topside needs no tying.)
3. Put the reserved bones and trimmings into a large, heavy pan. Place the beef on top, pour in enough cold water to cover and bring slowly to the boil. Remove the scum, cover the pan and simmer gently for 1½ hours.
4. Remove and discard the bones and trimmings. Add all the vegetables, bring to the boil again and simmer for another 1½ hours.
5. Lift out the meat and put it on a large, flat dish.

Put a board or a plate on top of it and weights on top. Allow to cool in the refrigerator for about 1 hour.

6. Measure 600 ml (1 pint) of the stock and boil, uncovered, in a small saucepan until reduced by half. Allow to cool and reserve for garnish.

7. Skim the remaining stock for soup. Strain the vegetables and put them through a sieve or food processor. Stir into the stock and taste for seasoning. Add 2-3 tablespoons of whisky if liked.

8. When the beef is almost cold remove the weights and plate and garnish the meat with finely sliced gherkins. Pour the reduced stock very gently over the beef so that the pattern of the gherkins is not disturbed. If the stock has already begun to gell, melt gently until it will pour. Refrigerate the garnished beef for at least another 2 hours.

*Pot roasted beef*

# CHAPTER FOUR

# HARVEST SUPPERS

These recipes provide hearty and wholesome dishes to enjoy by the fireside. They use combinations of vegetables or fruit or nuts and the more economic cuts of meat or dairy products to make warming soups, energy-restoring pasta dishes, nutritious pies or satisfying casseroles. Many of the dishes make a meal in themselves, others can be teamed with a simply-cooked vegetable or a quickly-prepared salad to become a substantial supper for all the family.

# LAMB, BARLEY AND VEGETABLE BROTH

450 g (1 lb) middle neck of lamb
1.2 litres (2 pints) water
salt
freshly ground black pepper
1 large carrot, peeled and diced
1 large parsnip, peeled and diced
1 large onion, peeled and chopped
1 large leek, sliced
40 g (1½ oz) pearl barley
1 tablespoon chopped fresh parsley, to garnish

*Preparation time: 15 minutes*
*Cooking time: 2-2½ hours*

1. Put the lamb into a large pan with the water, salt and pepper. Bring to the boil, skimming off any scum that rises to the surface and simmer for 1 hour.
2. Remove the pan from the heat. Take out the meat, remove and discard the bones. Cut the meat into cubes, then return it to the broth with the vegetables and barley.
3. Bring to the boil and simmer for a further 1-1½ hours. Sprinkle with chopped parsley, to garnish and serve with Brown Soda Bread (see page 124).

# CORN CHOWDER

25 g (1 oz) butter
1 medium onion, peeled and chopped
1 small green pepper, cored, seeded and sliced
100 g (4 oz) button mushrooms, sliced
1 tablespoon plain flour
300 ml (½ pint) light stock
300 ml (½ pint) milk
1 × 425 g (15 oz) can sweetcorn
2 medium potatoes, peeled and diced
salt
freshly ground black pepper
1 × 150 ml (¼ pint) carton single cream

*Preparation time: 10 minutes*
*Cooking time: 35 minutes*

1. Melt the butter in a pan, add the onion, pepper and mushrooms and cook for 2-3 minutes.
2. Stir in the flour and cook for 2 minutes, then add

the stock, milk, sweetcorn with the liquid from the can, potatoes, salt and pepper.
3. Bring to the boil and simmer for 30 minutes. Add the cream to the pan and reheat without boiling. Serve with granary rolls.

*Variation:*
When in season this soup can be made with fresh corn cobs. Boil them in unsalted water for 10-15 minutes, then scrape the corn from the husks with a sharp knife.

# PURÉE OF CELERY SOUP

*Serves 4-6*

50 g (2 oz) butter or margarine
450 g (1 lb) celery, cut into 1.5 cm (½ inch) pieces
225 g (8 oz) potatoes, peeled and cut into 2.5 cm (1 inch) dice
1.2 litres (2 pints) chicken stock or water
and 1 chicken stock cube
1 bouquet garni
salt
freshly ground pepper
150 ml (¼ pint) single cream
chopped fresh chervil or parsley, to garnish

*Preparation time: 20 minutes*
*Cooking time: 35-40 minutes*

1. Heat the butter or margarine in a large pan. Add the vegetables and toss.
2. Add the stock, or water and stock cube, the bouquet garni, salt and pepper. Simmer for 30 minutes.
3. Remove the herbs if desired, although these can be puréed with the other ingredients. Sieve, or purée the soup in a blender or food processor, return to the pan with the cream and heat. Serve garnished with the chopped herb.

*Variation:*
Celery and Tomato Purée: Use the recipe above but add 450 g (1 lb) skinned and chopped tomatoes and use 900 ml (1½ pints) stock only.

*Lamb, barley and vegetable broth*

# BUCKWHEAT SPAGHETTI WITH SPICED CHICKEN

225 g (8 oz) buckwheat spaghetti
salt
40 g (1½ oz) soft margarine
1 medium onion, peeled and finely chopped
1 garlic clove, peeled and finely chopped
1 teaspoon ground coriander
½ teaspoon ground cardamom
2 tablespoons wholewheat flour
150 ml (¼ pint) plain unsweetened yogurt
450 ml (¾ pint) chicken stock
350 g (12 oz) cooked chicken, diced
2 egg yolks
1 tablespoon chopped fresh parsley
100 g (4 oz) button mushrooms, thinly sliced
40 g (1½ oz) fresh wholewheat breadcrumbs
25 g (1 oz) grated Parmesan cheese
sprig of parsley, to garnish

*Preparation time: 20 minutes*
*Cooking time: 1 hour*
*Oven: 180°C, 350°F, Gas Mark 4*

1. Cook the spaghetti in plenty of boiling, salted water for about 12 minutes, or according to the directions on the packet, until it is just tender. Drain, refresh in hot water, and drain again.
2. Melt the margarine and fry the onion over moderate heat for 3 minutes, stirring frequently. Add the garlic, coriander and cardamom and cook for 1 minute. Stir in the flour and cook for 1 minute. Remove the pan from the heat and gradually stir in the yogurt, then the stock. Simmer for 3 minutes. Remove from the heat and allow to cool a little.
3. Stir in the chicken, egg yolks and parsley.
4. Spread half the spaghetti in a greased, shallow baking dish and cover with half the chicken sauce. Arrange the mushrooms on top and cover with the remaining spaghetti, then the sauce. Mix the breadcrumbs and cheese and sprinkle over the top.
5. Put the dish on a baking tray, place in a preheated oven and bake for 45 minutes. Serve hot, garnished with a sprig of parsley.

FROM THE TOP: *Mushroom and ham lasagne; Buckwheat spaghetti with spiced chicken*

# Mushroom and Ham Lasagne

*Serves 4-6*

225 g (8 oz) wholewheat lasagne
salt
2 tablespoons olive oil
1 large onion, peeled and chopped
225 g (8 oz) button mushrooms, thinly sliced
1 tablespoon flour
1 tablespoon lemon juice
300 ml (½ pint) plain unsweetened yogurt
freshly ground black pepper
75 g (3 oz) chopped walnuts
100 g (4 oz) lean ham, cut into matchstick strips
1 tablespoon chopped fresh parsley
*Sauce:*
300 ml (½ pint) plain unsweetened yogurt
175 g (6 oz) Wensleydale cheese, grated
6 tablespoons wholemeal breadcrumbs

*Preparation time: 40 minutes*
*Cooking time: 1 hour*
*Oven: 190°C, 375°F, Gas Mark 5*

1. Cook the lasagne sheets in plenty of boiling, salted water for about 15 minutes, or according to the directions on the packet, until it is just tender, stirring occasionally. Drain, rinse in cold water and drain again. Pat the sheets dry with kitchen paper.
2. Heat the oil and fry the onion over moderate heat for 3 minutes, stirring frequently. Add the mushrooms and cook for 2 minutes. Stir in the flour and cook for 1 minute. Remove the pan from the heat and gradually stir in the lemon juice and yogurt. Cook, stirring, until the mixture thickens, then season with salt and pepper. Simmer for 2 minutes. Stir in the walnuts, ham and parsley and remove from the heat.
3. Pour a layer of this sauce into a greased, shallow baking dish. Cover with sheets of lasagne and continue making layers, finishing with a layer of lasagne.
4. For the sauce, stir the yogurt and half the cheese together and pour over the dish. Sprinkle over the remaining cheese mixed with the breadcrumbs.
5. Stand the dish on a baking sheet. Place in a preheated oven and bake for 25-30 minutes, or until the top is deep brown and the sauce bubbling.

## AUBERGINE LAYER

1 medium aubergine, thinly sliced
salt
225 g (8 oz) wholewheat short-cut macaroni
4 tablespoons olive oil
350 g (12 oz) minced steak
350 g (12 oz) tomatoes, skinned and sliced
1 teaspoon dried oregano
1 tablespoon chopped fresh parsley
freshly ground black pepper
100 g (4 oz) Wensleydale cheese, very thinly sliced
100 g (4 oz) button mushrooms, thinly sliced
50 g (2 oz) fresh wholewheat breadcrumbs
50 g (2 oz) grated Parmesan cheese

*Preparation time: 30 minutes, plus draining*
*Cooking time: 1¼ hours*
*Oven: 180°C, 350°F, Gas Mark 4*

1. Put the aubergine slices in a colander over a dish and sprinkle with salt. Leave to drain for 30 minutes, then rinse thoroughly. Drain the slices and pat dry with kitchen paper.
2. Meanwhile, cook the macaroni in plenty of boiling, salted water for about 12 minutes, or according to the directions on the packet, until it is just tender. Drain, refresh in hot water, and drain again.
3. Heat the oil in a pan and fry the aubergine slices, a few at a time, over moderate heat for 5 minutes for each batch. Remove from the pan as they are cooked and keep hot.
4. Fry the meat in the pan for 6 minutes, stirring frequently. Stir in the tomatoes and herbs and cook for 10 minutes. Season with salt and pepper.
5. In a greased, shallow baking dish make layers of the macaroni, aubergines, meat sauce, sliced cheese and mushrooms, finishing with the aubergine. Mix together the breadcrumbs and Parmesan cheese and sprinkle over the top. [F]
6. Put the dish on a baking sheet. Place in a preheated oven and bake for 45 minutes. Serve hot with a green salad.

[F] Freeze the uncooked dish for up to 2 months. Thaw in the refrigerator overnight, or bake from frozen for 1 hour.

## PASTA TWISTS WITH BROCCOLI SPEARS

350 g (12 oz) pasta twists, bows, or other shapes
salt
450 g (1 lb) broccoli spears
1 tablespoon olive oil
15 g (½ oz) butter
1 small onion, peeled and finely chopped
40 g (1½ oz) walnuts, roughly chopped
40 g (1½ oz) anchovy fillets, chopped
1 tablespoon chopped fresh parsley
freshly ground black pepper
25 g (1 oz) grated Parmesan cheese

*Preparation time: 20 minutes*
*Cooking time: 30 minutes*

1. Cook the pasta in plenty of boiling, salted water for 15 minutes, or according to the directions on the packet, until it is just tender. Drain, refresh in hot water, then drain once more.
2. Blanch the broccoli by cooking it in boiling, salted water for 5 minutes. Drain, then plunge at once into cold water to prevent further cooking. Drain again.
3. Heat the oil with the butter and fry the onion over low heat for 10 minutes, stirring occasionally.
4. Next, stir in the walnuts, anchovies and broccoli and cook slowly over gentle heat for 3-4 minutes.
5. Stir in the pasta and heat through. Remove from the heat, add the parsley, season well with pepper and stir in the cheese. Serve at once.

## GREEN NOODLES WITH BLUE CHEESE

350 g (12 oz) green spinach noodles,
or other pasta shapes
salt
6 rashers streaky bacon, rinded and chopped
225 g (8 oz) cottage cheese
50 g (2 oz) Roquefort cheese, crumbled
2 spring onions, thinly sliced
freshly ground black pepper

*Preparation time: 15 minutes*
*Cooking time: 15 minutes*

1. Cook the noodles in plenty of boiling, salted water until they are just tender. Drain, refresh in hot water, and drain again. Keep hot.
2. Fry the bacon over moderate heat until the fat has run and the bacon is crispy. Remove with a slotted spoon and reserve.
3. Toss the noodles with the cheeses and onions and season with salt and pepper. Stir in the bacon.
4. Turn the noodles into a heated serving dish. Serve at once.

CLOCKWISE FROM TOP LEFT: *Aubergine layer; Pasta twists with broccoli spears; Green noodles with blue cheese*

# BACON AND POTATO HOT POT

20 g (¼ oz) butter, for greasing
750 g (1½ lb) peeled potatoes, thickly sliced
salt
freshly ground black pepper
450 g (1 lb) thickly sliced smoked bacon, rinded
2 tablespoons chopped fresh parsley
2 medium onions, peeled and thinly sliced
600 ml (1 pint) chicken stock

*Preparation time: 35 minutes*
*Cooking time: 2 hours*
*Oven: 120°C, 250°F, Gas Mark 1/2*

1. Grease a large casserole dish with 1 tablespoon of the butter. Place a third of the potato slices on the bottom of the dish. Add the salt and pepper. Top with half of the bacon. Sprinkle half of the parsley on the bacon. Add half of the onion slices. Season with salt and pepper. Place a third of the potato slices over the onion. Add the salt and pepper. Repeat the layers with the remaining bacon, parsley and onion slices and put the remaining potatoes in an overlapping layer on top. Add salt and pepper. Pour the stock into the casserole dish. Grease a sheet of greaseproof paper with the remaining butter. Cover the casserole dish with the paper, then the lid. A Place in a preheated oven and cook for 1½ hours.
2. Remove the lid and greaseproof paper from the casserole. Return the casserole to the oven and cook for 20-30 minutes, until the top is brown.

A Can be prepared several hours in advance, covered and kept chilled.

TOP: *Bacon and potato hot pot;*
BOTTOM: *Braised stuffed pork chops*

# BRAISED STUFFED PORK CHOPS

*Serves 6*

6 pork chops, about 175 g (6 oz) each, 2.5 cm
(1 inch) thick and fat trimmed
salt
freshly ground black pepper
100 g (4 oz) dried breadcrumbs
1 small onion, peeled and finely chopped
1 stick celery, finely sliced
1 garlic clove, peeled and finely chopped
2 tablespoons finely chopped fresh parsley
1 egg, beaten
¼ teaspoon paprika
2 tablespoons vegetable oil
650 ml (22 fl oz) chicken stock
120 ml (4 fl oz) white wine
2 tablespoons cornflour
120 ml (4 fl oz) double or whipping cream
bunch watercress, to garnish

*Preparation time: 25 minutes*
*Cooking time: 1¾ hours*
*Oven: 180°C, 350°F, Gas Mark 4*

1. Cut a pocket in the side of the pork chops for the stuffing. Do not cut all the way through. Sprinkle the chops with salt and pepper, then set aside.
2. Combine the breadcrumbs, onion, celery, garlic, parsley, egg, paprika, salt and pepper in a medium bowl. Stuff the pork chops with this mixture. Use metal skewers or wooden toothpicks to enclose the stuffing. Set aside.
3. Heat the oil in a flameproof casserole over a medium-high heat. Add the pork chops and brown on one side for 6-7 minutes. Turn the chops over and brown the other side for 4-5 minutes. Remove the chops from the casserole with tongs or a slotted spoon and set aside. Drain the excess fat from the casserole and discard.
4. Add 600 ml (1 pint) of the stock and the wine to the casserole, scraping the bottom to incorporate all the bits. When the stock mixture comes to the boil, return the pork chops to the casserole. Cover and place in a preheated oven. Cook for 1¼ hours.
5. Remove the casserole from the oven. Transfer the chops to a heated serving platter and keep warm. Place the casserole over a high heat. Combine the cornflour and the remaining stock in a cup, stirring until smooth. Using a whisk, blend into the casserole. Bring to the boil, stirring constantly. Stir the cream into the casserole. Taste and adjust the seasoning, if necessary.
6. To serve, pour the sauce over the chops, then garnish with the watercress.

***Stuffing variations:***
For *prune stuffing*, omit the garlic and paprika. Soak 6 prunes in enough water to cover for 1 hour. Drain, stone and chop the prunes. Add them and ¼ teaspoon crumbled dried rosemary to the stuffing.

For *apple stuffing*, one small cooking apple, cored and finely chopped, and 50 g (2 oz) raisins may be added to the original stuffing.

For *sausage stuffing*, crumble 100 g (4 oz) sausage meat into a small frying pan and cook for 10 minutes, stirring frequently to break up the pieces, until browned and cooked through. Drain off any excess fat and add the sausage meat to the original stuffing.

With both the apple and sausage stuffings, any leftover stuffing can be placed in a small oven-proof dish and cooked for 20 minutes alongside the chops.

# OVEN POTATO OMELETTE

50 g (2 oz) butter or margarine
2 large cooked potatoes, sliced
2 canned red peppers, diced
6-8 eggs
2 tablespoons single cream or milk
salt
1 tablespoon chopped chives
1 tablespoon chopped fresh parsley
1 teaspoon grated lemon rind

*Preparation time: 15 minutes*
*Cooking time: 20-25 minutes*
*Oven: 220°C, 425°F, Gas Mark 7*

1. Put the butter or margarine into a 20-23 cm (8-9 inch) round ovenproof dish and heat towards the top of a preheated hot oven until melted. Add the potatoes and peppers and heat for another 5 minutes.
2. Beat the eggs with the remaining ingredients, pour over the potato and pepper mixture and return to the oven just above the centre.
3. Bake for 10 to 15 minutes, or until set to personal taste.

# SAUSAGE AND APPLE CASSEROLE

25 g (1 oz) butter
750 g (1½ lb) pork sausages
1 medium onion, peeled and chopped
2 tablespoons demerara sugar
½ teaspoon allspice
salt
freshly ground black pepper
2 cooking apples, cored and sliced
*To finish:*
25 g (1 oz) butter
25 g (1 oz) plain flour
600 ml (1 pint) beef stock
1 tablespoon finely chopped fresh parsley,
to garnish

*Preparation time: 15 minutes*
*Cooking time: 1 hour*
*Oven: 190°C, 375°F, Gas Mark 5*

1. Melt all but 1 tablespoon of the butter in a large frying pan over a moderate heat. Add the sausages and brown for 5 minutes, turning frequently. Remove the sausages with a pair of tongs to drain on paper towels. Set aside.
2. Add the onion to the frying pan. Cook for 5 minutes over a moderate heat, stirring frequently. Remove the onion with a slotted spoon and set aside. Reserve the fat in the pan.
3. Grease a large casserole with the remaining butter. Arrange the sausages in the casserole. Sprinkle with a third of the sugar, allspice, salt and pepper. Top with the onion. Sprinkle with a third of the sugar, allspice, salt and pepper. Arrange the apple slices over the onion. Season with the remaining sugar, allspice, salt and pepper.
4. To finish, melt the butter in a small saucepan over a moderate heat. Add the flour and cook for 2-3 minutes, stirring constantly. Using a whisk, gradually stir in the stock. Bring the mixture to the boil, stirring constantly, and cook until smooth and thickened. Pour the sauce over the casserole. [A]
5. Cover and place in a preheated oven. Cook for 45 minutes. Serve sprinkled with the parsley.

[A] Can be prepared several hours in advance, then covered and kept chilled. Stand at room temperature for 1 hour before proceeding with the recipe.

# CHICORY AND HAM ROLLS GOURMET

1 tablespoon butter, for greasing
2.25 litres (4 pints) water
2 tablespoons lemon juice
12 heads chicory, bases trimmed
12 slices thin ham
¼ teaspoon freshly ground nutmeg
salt
freshly ground black pepper
2 hard-boiled eggs, shelled and sliced
*Sauce:*
50 g (2 oz) butter
50 g (2 oz) plain flour
475 ml (16 fl oz) milk
100 g (4 oz) Edam cheese, grated
*Topping:*
25 g (1 oz) buttered breadcrumbs
25 g (1 oz) Edam cheese, grated

*Preparation time: 15 minutes*
*Cooking time: 55 minutes*
*Oven: 190°C, 375°F, Gas Mark 5*

1. Grease a medium casserole with the butter, then set aside.
2. Bring the water and lemon juice to a simmer in a large saucepan. Add the chicory and lower the heat. Cook for 10 minutes until the heads are tender but still firm. Drain the chicory.
3. Wrap each head of chicory in a slice of ham and arrange the rolls in the casserole. Sprinkle with the nutmeg, salt and pepper. Top with the egg slices. Cover and set aside.
4. For the sauce, melt the butter in a medium saucepan over a moderate heat. Blend in the flour. Cook for 2-3 minutes, stirring constantly. Using a whisk, gradually stir in the milk. Cook, stirring constantly, until smooth and thick. Add the cheese and cook until just melted. Remove the saucepan from the heat, then add salt and pepper to taste. Pour the sauce over the casserole.
5. For the topping, sprinkle the casserole with the buttered breadcrumbs and cheese. [A]
6. Cook in a preheated oven for 35 minutes. Serve with a tomato salad.

[A] Can be prepared several hours in advance, covered and kept chilled. Stand at room temperature for 1 hour before proceeding with the recipe.

CLOCKWISE FROM TOP LEFT: *Sausage and apple casserole; Courgette and bacon casserole; Chicory and ham rolls gourmet*

# COURGETTE AND BACON CASSEROLE

*Serves 6*

2.25 litres (4 pints) water
1 kg (2 lb) small courgettes, sliced
4 eggs, beaten
450 ml (¾ pint) milk
250 g (8 oz) Cheddar cheese, grated
¼ teaspoon paprika
salt
freshly ground black pepper
1 tablespoon butter, for greasing
100 g (4 oz) streaky bacon, grilled until crisp and crumbled

*Preparation time: 30 minutes*
*Cooking time: 1 hour*
*Oven: 180°C, 350°F, Gas Mark 4*

1. Bring the water to the boil in a large saucepan over a high heat. Add the courgettes and cook for 2 minutes. Drain the courgettes in a colander under cold running water. Shake the colander well to remove excess water.
2. Combine the eggs and milk in a large bowl. Stir in 150 g (5 oz) of the cheese. Add the paprika, salt and pepper.
3. Grease a medium casserole dish with the butter. Place half of the courgettes in the dish. Sprinkle the courgettes with the bacon. Top with the remaining courgettes. Pour the egg mixture into the casserole. Sprinkle with the remaining cheese. A
4. Place in a preheated oven and cook for 35-40 minutes until set and the top is golden brown. Serve with a mixed salad and hot bread.

A Can be prepared several hours in advance, then covered and kept chilled. Allow to stand at room temperature for 1 hour before proceeding with the recipe.

# LEEK OR LIKKY PIE

225 g (8 oz) flaky pastry (page 38)
6 large leeks, washed, trimmed and cut into
1 cm (½ inch) lengths
2 eggs, beaten
150 ml (¼ pint) double or whipping cream
150 ml (¼ pint) milk
100 g (4 oz) streaky bacon or pork,
rinded and finely chopped
salt
freshly ground black pepper

*Preparation time: 30 minutes, plus chilling*
*Cooking time: 45 minutes*
*Oven: 200°C, 400°F, Gas Mark 6*

1. Chill the pastry for 30-40 minutes.
2. Put the leeks into boiling, salted water and cook for about 7 minutes, then drain well.
3. Reserve a little of the egg for glazing, then beat in the rest with the cream and milk.
4. Put the leeks, bacon, eggs and cream into a deep pie dish and season to taste.
5. Dampen the edges of the pie dish, roll out the pastry to the size of the dish and put on top, pinching the edges well. Brush over with the reserved beaten egg and bake for about half an hour.

# PARSON'S HAT

This is a Devonshire version of the pasty.

225 g (8 oz) shortcrust pastry (see right)
4 tablespoons white sauce, or 2 eggs beaten with
2 tablespoons milk
225 g (8 oz) cooked haddock, salmon, cod, etc.
pinch of cayenne pepper
salt
freshly ground black pepper
1 tablespoon grated Cheddar cheese
milk, for brushing

*Preparation time: 45 minutes, plus chilling*
*Cooking time: 30 minutes*
*Oven: 190°C, 375°F, Gas Mark 5*

1. Chill the pastry for 30-40 minutes.
2. Put the sauce or egg mixture into a basin. Take all the skin and bones from the fish and mix with the sauce or egg. Season well with cayenne, salt and pepper, and add the cheese.
3. Roll out the pastry fairly thinly and cut into 8-10 cm (3-4 inch) circles. Brush with a little of the egg and milk and divide the filling between the rounds. Slightly dampen the edges and press upwards into a three-cornered shape with a little filling showing at the top.
4. Put on to a lightly greased baking tray and brush over with a little milk. Place in a preheated oven and bake for about half an hour.

# PRIDDY OGGIES

Oggie is a West Country name for pastry. Priddy oggies, with a meat and cheese filling, were first served at The Miner's Arms, in Priddy, Somerset.

*Makes 8*

25 g (1 oz) butter
25 g (1 oz) lard
1 small egg yolk
90 g (3½ oz) Cheddar cheese, grated
2½ tablespoons water
pinch of salt
225 g (8 oz) plain flour, sifted
600 ml (1 pint) vegetable oil, for deep frying
*Filling:*
500 g (1¼ lb) pork fillet
1 egg, beaten
75 g (3 oz) mature Cheddar cheese, grated
2 tablespoons chopped fresh parsley
pinch of salt
a little cayenne pepper
40 g (1½ oz) smoked bacon, cut into 8 strips

*Preparation time: 60 minutes, plus chilling*
*Cooking time: about 25 minutes*
*Oven: 200°C, 400°F, Gas Mark 6*

1. To make the pastry, mix all the ingredients except the flour in a warm bowl until soft. Chill the mixture in a refrigerator until it is firm. Sieve the flour and rub in the cooled mixture roughly.
2. Divide the mixture into thirds. Take each piece and roll it 2 or 3 times into a 1 cm (½ inch) slab, moistening the top of each slab slightly before laying them on top of each other. When finished, press down firmly and cut downwards into 3 pieces, repeating the rolling process twice more. Chill for 30 minutes.

*3.* Trim the fillet and slice lengthways into two, then beat gently until flat.

*4.* Reserve half the beaten egg, then place the cheese, parsley, salt and cayenne in the bowl with the rest of the egg and mix well.

*5.* Spread the mixture evenly over the cut sides of the pork fillet, then roll up each piece, pressing down firmly. Chill for 30 minutes.

*6.* To assemble the oggies, cut each roll of fillet into 4 slices and wrap them round with a piece of bacon. Roll out the pastry and cut into 8 equal squares. Lay a slice of the stuffed meat in the centre of the pastry, then moisten around the edges with a little water. Bring the pastry up and over the meat, pressing the edges together in a scalloped design. Press down the base slightly to flatten. Put onto a baking sheet and when all are ready brush over with the remaining beaten egg.

*7.* Place the oggies in the centre of a preheated oven and bake for about 15 minutes, or until they are just starting to brown.

*8.* Heat the oil in a deep fryer to 180°C/350°F, or until a cube of bread browns in 30 seconds. Deep-fry the oggies until the pastry begins to brown, then drain on paper towels.

FROM THE TOP: *Leek or likky pie; Priddy oggies; Parson's hat*

# Shortcrust Pastry

¼ teaspoon salt
450 g (1 lb) plain flour
225 g (8 oz) butter or margarine
6 tablespoons iced water

*1.* Make the pastry by sifting the salt and flour, then rub in the fat with the fingers until it is like coarse breadcrumbs.

*2.* Add enough iced water gradually to make a stiff dough, kneading lightly with your hands until it is smooth.

*3.* Wrap up the pastry in polythene and chill for at least 30 minutes before rolling out.

# PAPRIKA PORK CHOPS

45 g (1¼ oz) plain flour
2 tablespoons paprika
¼ teaspoon cayenne
salt
freshly ground black pepper
4 loin pork chops, 175 g (6 oz) each
1 tablespoon vegetable oil
4 medium potatoes, peeled and thinly sliced
1 large onion, peeled and thinly sliced
300 ml (½ pint) beef stock
300 ml (½ pint) soured cream
*To garnish:*
1 bunch watercress
1 teaspoon caraway seeds (optional)

*Preparation time: 25 minutes*
*Cooking time: 1 hour*
*Oven: 190°C, 375°F, Gas Mark 5*

1. Combine 25 g (1 oz) of the flour, the paprika, cayenne, salt and pepper on a large plate. Coat the pork chops in this mixture.
2. Heat the oil in a large flameproof casserole over a moderate heat. Add the pork chops and brown for 10 minutes, turning frequently. Remove the chops with tongs and set aside.
3. Lay the potato and onion slices on the bottom of the casserole. Place the pork chops on top of the slices. Pour the stock into the casserole. Cover and place in a preheated oven. Cook for 45 minutes.
4. Combine the soured cream and remaining flour until smooth. Set aside.
5. Remove the pork chops and vegetables from the casserole. Arrange on a heated serving platter and keep warm. Place the casserole over a medium-low heat. Using a whisk, stir in the soured cream mixture. Cook until just heated through. Remove the sauce from the heat and pour over the chops. Garnish with the watercress and caraway seeds, if using, then serve immediately.

FROM THE TOP: *Paprika pork chops; Orange and liver casserole; Cider pork chops*

# ORANGE AND LIVER CASSEROLE

25 g (1 oz) plain flour
salt
freshly ground black pepper
1 kg (2 lb) lamb's liver, thinly sliced
40 g (1½ oz) butter
2 tablespoons vegetable oil
1 medium onion, peeled and thinly sliced
1 garlic clove, peeled and finely chopped
2 oranges, thinly sliced and seeds removed
250 ml (8 fl oz) dry red wine
250 ml (8 fl oz) orange juice
2 tablespoons orange marmalade
2 tablespoons fresh thyme leaves or
1 teaspoon dried thyme
2 tablespoons double cream
1 tablespoon finely chopped fresh parsley,
to garnish

*Preparation time: 20 minutes*
*Cooking time: 45 minutes*
*Oven: 140°C, 275°F, Gas Mark 1*

The liver for this recipe should be very thinly sliced. The fresh liver sold in some butchers' shops is not sliced thinly enough, so you may prefer to buy frozen liver. When it has partially thawed, carefully slice it with a sharp knife.

1. Combine the flour, salt and pepper on a large plate. Coat the liver with the flour, shaking off the excess. Set aside.
2. Heat the butter and oil in a large frying pan over a moderate heat. Add the onion and garlic, then cook for 5 minutes, stirring occasionally. Transfer the onion and garlic with a slotted spoon to a large casserole and set aside.
3. Add the liver slices to the frying pan. Cook on one side for 2-3 minutes until brown, then turn the slices over. Cook on the other side for 2 minutes. Transfer the liver with a slotted spoon to the casserole and set aside.
4. Add the orange slices to the frying pan. Cook for 1-2 minutes, turning frequently. Transfer the orange slices with a slotted spoon over the liver in the casserole and set aside.
5. Add the wine, orange juice, marmalade, thyme, salt and pepper to the frying pan. Bring to the boil, stirring constantly, then pour over the ingredients in the casserole.
6. Cover and place the casserole in a preheated oven. Cook for 30 minutes.
7. Remove the casserole from the oven and stir in the cream. Garnish with the parsley.

# CIDER PORK CHOPS

4 loin pork chops, 175 g (6 oz) each
salt
freshly ground black pepper
2 tablespoons vegetable oil
15 g (½ oz) butter
1 medium onion, peeled and thinly sliced
1 cooking apple, cored and chopped
225 g (8 oz) button mushrooms, cleaned and sliced
1 large garlic clove, peeled and finely chopped
1 tablespoon fresh thyme leaves
or ½ teaspoon dried thyme
1 tablespoon finely chopped fresh rosemary
or ½ teaspoon dried rosemary
350 ml (12 fl oz) dry cider
150 ml (¼ pint) double cream

*Preparation time: 15 minutes*
*Cooking time: 1¼ hours*

1. Season the pork chops with the salt and pepper.
2. Heat the oil and butter in a flameproof casserole over a moderate heat. Add the pork chops and brown on both sides for 10 minutes, turning frequently. Using a pair of tongs, remove the chops from the casserole and set aside.
3. Add the onion, apple, mushrooms and garlic to the casserole. Cook over a moderate heat for 5 minutes, stirring frequently. Push the mixture to one side of the casserole. Return the chops to the casserole. Add the thyme and rosemary. Spoon the onion mixture over the chops, then add the cider. Reduce the heat to low and cover. Simmer for 45 minutes.
4. Remove the cover and transfer the chops to a heated serving platter. Keep warm. Raise the heat under the casserole to moderate. Stir in the cream. Bring the sauce to a simmer and let it reduce slightly, stirring frequently. Taste the sauce and adjust the seasoning, if necessary.
5. To serve, pour the sauce over the chops.

# LAMB CHOPS WITH CHESTNUTS

Gather fresh chestnuts in October, November and December and try them in this simple dish of chops.

4 lamb loin chops, trimmed
2 tablespoons plain flour
50 g (2 oz) butter
2 large onions, peeled and finely sliced
750 g (1½ lb) chestnuts, peeled, skinned and boiled until just tender
450 ml (¾ pint) beef stock
300 ml (½ pint) red wine
¼ teaspoon ground mace
½ teaspoon dried thyme
½ teaspoon salt
¼ teaspoon freshly ground black pepper

*Preparation time: 40 minutes*
*Cooking time: 2¼ hours*
*Oven: 150°C, 300°F, Gas Mark 2*

1. Sprinkle the chops with the flour. Heat the butter in a large frying pan, add the chops and fry briskly for 2 minutes on each side.
2. Transfer the chops to a fairly deep casserole. Fry the onions in the same butter for about 5 minutes, until soft and transparent, then scatter over the chops. Add the chestnuts.
3. Mix together the stock, wine, mace, thyme, salt and pepper and pour over the chops. Cover and cook in a preheated oven for 2 hours, or until the chops are tender and cooked through.

FROM THE LEFT: *Lamb chops with chestnuts; Fricassée of pork with apple rings*

# FRICASSÉE OF PORK WITH APPLE RINGS

750 g (1½ lb) pork fillet, trimmed
3 tablespoons plain flour
salt
freshly ground black pepper
50 g (2 oz) butter
1 large onion, peeled and thinly sliced
300 ml (½ pint) hot chicken stock
300 ml (½ pint) milk
1 bay leaf
1 sprig each fresh thyme, parsley, marjoram or
1 bouquet garni
*Apple rings:*
25 g (1 oz) butter
2 dessert apples, peeled, cored and cut across in 5 mm (¼ inch) rings

*Preparation time: 20 minutes*
*Cooking time: 45 minutes*

1. Cut the pork into neat pieces about 5 × 2.5 cm (2 × 1 inch) and 5 mm (¼ inch) thick. Season 2 table-spoons of the flour with ¼ teaspoon each of salt and pepper and place in a polythene bag. Add the pork and shake until thoroughly coated.
2. Melt half the butter in a flameproof casserole, add the onion and fry gently for about 5 minutes until soft but not coloured. Transfer to a plate and set aside.
3. In the same pan fry the pork, adding a little more butter if necessary, for 2 minutes on each side, until lightly browned. Transfer to the plate with the onion.
4. Stir the remaining flour into the casserole, scrap-ing down the sides with a wooden spoon. Cook for 1-2 minutes. Gradually stir in the chicken stock and finally stir in the milk. Cook for 2-3 minutes, stirring, until thickened and smooth.
5. Stir the herbs into the sauce, then put in the pork and the onions. Cover and simmer very gently for 30 minutes, until the pork is tender.
6. Meanwhile, melt 25 g (1 oz) butter in a frying pan, add the apple rings and fry gently for 2 or 3 min-utes on each side.
7. Remove the herbs from the casserole, taste and adjust the seasoning, if necessary, arrange the apple rings round the edge of the casserole and serve.

# BRAISED CHICKEN WITH NEW POTATOES AND PAPRIKA

2 tablespoons vegetable oil
200 g (7 oz) streaky bacon, rinded and cut into strips
1 × 1½ kg (3 lb) chicken, cut into 8 pieces
salt
freshly ground black pepper
1 large onion, peeled and chopped
1 large green pepper, cored, seeded and chopped
1 garlic clove, peeled and finely chopped
4 tablespoons plain flour
2 tablespoons sweet paprika
600 ml (1 pint) chicken stock
120 ml (4 fl oz) dry white wine
12 small red or white new potatoes, halved
300 ml (½ pint) soured cream

*Preparation time: 25 minutes*
*Cooking time: 1¼ hours*

1. Heat the oil in a large flameproof casserole over a moderate heat. Add the bacon and cook for 5 minutes, stirring frequently. Remove the bacon with a slotted spoon and set aside. Pour off all but 3 tablespoons of the fat.
2. Season the chicken pieces with the salt and pepper. Place in the casserole, skin side down, over a medium-high heat. Brown, turning occasionally, for 10-15 minutes. Remove the chicken with tongs and set aside.
3. Place the onion in the casserole over a medium heat. Cook, stirring occasionally, for 5 minutes. Add the pepper and garlic, then cook for 1 minute. Blend in 2 tablespoons of the flour and the paprika and cook for 2-3 minutes, stirring constantly. Using a whisk, gradually blend in the stock and wine. Bring the mixture to the boil and cook until the sauce is smooth and thick.
4. Return the chicken and bacon to the sauce. Arrange the potatoes around the chicken. Cover and cook over a medium-low heat for 30 minutes. Remove the breast pieces from the casserole and keep warm on a heated serving platter. Continue cooking the dark meat pieces for another 10 minutes.
5. Remove the remaining chicken pieces and place on the serving platter. Keep warm. Test the potatoes. If they are not tender, cover the casserole and cook over a medium-low heat until they are cooked. Remove the potatoes with a slotted spoon and arrange around the chicken pieces.
6. To finish the sauce, reduce the heat to very low. Combine the soured cream and remaining flour in a small bowl until smooth. Using a whisk, stir into the sauce. Cook gently for 2 minutes.
7. Pour the sauce over the chicken and potatoes.

CLOCKWISE FROM TOP LEFT: *Turkey hash; Braised chicken with new potatoes and paprika; Somerset chicken*

# TURKEY HASH

A good dish for the week between Christmas and the New Year

*Serves 6*

40 g (1½ oz) butter
1 medium onion, peeled and finely chopped
1 red pepper, cored, seeded and diced
225 g (8 oz) button mushrooms, cleaned and sliced
1 garlic clove, peeled and finely chopped
450 g (1 lb) cooked turkey meat, cubed
275 g (10 oz) leftover turkey stuffing, cubed
300 ml (½ pint) double or whipping cream
250 ml (8 fl oz) turkey or chicken stock
120 ml (4 fl oz) leftover turkey gravy
2 tablespoons cornflour
15 g (½ oz) finely chopped fresh parsley
⅛ teaspoon ground nutmeg
salt
freshly ground black pepper
25 g (1 oz) Gruyère cheese, grated

*Preparation time: 25 minutes*
*Cooking time: 50 minutes*
*Oven: 180°C, 350°F, Gas Mark 4*

1. Melt the butter in a medium flameproof casserole over a moderate heat. Add the onion and cook, stirring frequently, for 5 minutes. Add the pepper, mushrooms and garlic. Cook for 3 minutes, until the mushrooms begin to soften. Add the turkey and stuffing, then cook for 5 minutes, stirring occasionally. Remove the casserole from the heat and set aside.
2. Combine the cream, 175 ml (6 fl oz) of the stock and the gravy in a medium saucepan. Bring to the boil over a high heat. Combine the cornflour and the remaining stock in a cup until smooth and, using a whisk, stir into the sauce. Simmer for 2-3 minutes, stirring constantly, until smooth and thick. Remove from the heat and add the parsley, nutmeg, salt and pepper. Blend the sauce into the casserole, then sprinkle over the cheese. [A] Cover the casserole, place in a preheated oven and cook for 25 minutes until heated through.
3. Serve with crisp toast and a green salad.

[A] The casserole can be prepared in the morning, covered and kept chilled. Cook for 30 minutes until heated through.

# SOMERSET CHICKEN

4 tablespoons plain flour
salt
freshly ground black pepper
4 boneless chicken breasts, about 150 g (5 oz) each, skinned and cut into bite-sized pieces
1 medium onion, peeled and finely chopped
175 g (6 oz) button mushrooms, cleaned and sliced
2 tablespoons finely chopped fresh parsley
2 teaspoons mixed dried herbs
1 kg (2 lb) potatoes, peeled and thinly sliced
300 ml (½ pint) chicken stock
300 ml (½ pint) dry cider
chopped fresh parsley, to garnish

*Preparation time: 25 minutes*
*Cooking time: 1¼ hours*
*Oven: 190°C, 375°F, Gas Mark 5*

1. Place the flour, salt and pepper in a plastic bag. Add the chicken pieces and tightly seal the opening of the bag. Shake well to coat the chicken thoroughly. Transfer the chicken pieces to a large casserole.
2. Add the onion, mushrooms, parsley, herbs, salt and pepper to the casserole.
3. Arrange the potatoes on the top of the casserole. Pour in the chicken stock and cider. The potatoes should just be covered with liquid. [A] Cover the casserole and place in a preheated oven. Cook for 1 hour.
4. Take the lid off the casserole and cook for 15 minutes, until the top is brown.
5. Garnish with the parsley and serve with a green vegetable.

[A] Can be prepared several hours in advance, covered and kept chilled.

# TURKEY RICE CASSEROLE

50 g (2 oz) butter
2 medium onions, peeled and chopped
225 g (8 oz) button mushrooms, cleaned and sliced
225 g (8 oz) cooked turkey, cubed
150 g (5 oz) stuffing, cubed or crumbled
100 g (4 oz) ham, diced
2 tablespoons finely chopped fresh parsley
½ tablespoon fresh thyme leaves or ½ teaspoon dried thyme
salt
freshly ground black pepper
200 g (7 oz) long-grain rice
1 tablespoon mild curry powder
475 ml (16 fl oz) hot turkey or chicken stock

*Preparation time: 25 minutes*
*Cooking time: 1 hour*
*Oven: 190°C, 375°F, Gas Mark 5*

This is another good recipe for that perennial holiday problem – what to do with the left-over turkey and stuffing. This one is easy on the cook and has a mildly exotic flavour. Use homemade stuffing, not a packaged version.

1. Melt 40 g (1½ oz) of the butter in a large saucepan over a moderate heat. Add the onions and cook for 5 minutes, stirring frequently. Add the mushrooms and continue to cook for another 5 minutes, stirring frequently. Place the vegetable mixture in a medium casserole. Add the turkey, stuffing, ham, parsley, thyme, salt and pepper, then stir well to combine. Set aside.
2. In the saucepan used to cook the onions, melt the remaining butter over a moderate heat. Add the rice and curry powder. Brown, stirring frequently, for 5 minutes. Remove the pan from the heat and stir the mixture into the casserole. Pour in the hot stock and cover. Transfer to a preheated oven and cook for 40 minutes, until the rice is tender and the stock is absorbed.
3. Serve with chutney and a minted cucumber-yogurt salad.

*Turkey rice casserole*

*Chicken liver casserole*

# CHICKEN LIVER CASSEROLE

100 g (4 oz) butter
450 g (1 lb) chicken livers
1 medium onion,
peeled and finely chopped
100 g (4 oz) button mushrooms,
cleaned and thinly sliced
15 g (½ oz) plain flour
450 ml (¾ pint) milk
2 tablespoons finely chopped fresh parsley
salt
freshly ground black pepper
2 red peppers, cored, seeded and cut into rings

*Preparation time: 15 minutes*
*Cooking time: 45 minutes*
*Oven: 180°C, 350°F, Gas Mark 4*

1. Melt all but 15 g (½ oz) of the butter in a medium frying pan over a moderate heat. Add the livers and cook for 5 minutes, stirring frequently, until brown. Remove the livers from the pan with a slotted spoon and set aside.
2. Add the onion and mushrooms to the pan. Cook over a moderate heat for 5 minutes, stirring frequently. Blend in the flour. Cook for 2-3 minutes, stirring constantly. Using a whisk, gradually stir in the milk. Cook, stirring constantly, until the sauce is smooth and thick. Add the parsley, salt and pepper, then remove the sauce from the heat.
3. Grease a medium casserole with the remaining butter. Arrange the livers in the casserole. Top with the pepper rings. Pour the sauce over the casserole. A
4. Cover and place in a preheated oven. Cook for 30 minutes until hot. Serve the casserole with steamed rice and crisp stir-fried vegetables.

A Can be prepared 1 hour in advance and covered.

# CHAPTER FIVE

# THE FRUIT GARDEN

Plums, peaches and nectarines picked off the trees; apples and pears from the orchard; soft fruit quickly gathered in its short season; rich cream and yogurt from the dairy: these are the ingredients, home produced in the country, which make up this refreshing collection of jellies, ices, creams and puddings. From a selection of juicy, fresh fruits come these light and airy desserts for summer, as well as the hot, baked dishes for winter.

# STONE CREAM WITH PEACHES

*Stone cream with peaches*

Stone cream is an old English traditional dessert, usually with jam underneath. This version uses fresh peaches as a delicious alternative, although any fresh soft fruit can be used.

2 ripe peaches, stoned, skinned and sliced
50 g (2 oz) ratafia biscuits
3 teaspoons powdered gelatine
3 tablespoons water
300 ml (½ pint) cold milk
15 g (½ oz) caster sugar
150 ml (¼ pint) double or whipping cream, whipped
1 egg white
4 ratafia biscuits, to decorate

*Preparation time: 15 minutes, plus setting*
*Cooking time: 5 minutes*

1. Divide the peaches and ratafias between 4 dessert dishes.
2. Dissolve the gelatine in the water. Heat the milk and sugar in a small pan until the sugar has dissolved. Stir in the gelatine. Chill until cold and starting to set, about 30 minutes.
3. Fold the cream into the milk. Whisk the egg white until stiff and fold into the cream mixture. Pour over the peaches and ratafias. Decorate with ratafias. Leave until set.

**Variation:**
In winter the fresh fruit can be substituted with canned or frozen fruit.

# GLAZED GOOSEBERRY BOATS

The good old English gardeners always say that gooseberries are ready to pick at Whitsuntide, but, as this is a movable feast, no-one quite knows how they work this saying out! However the main crop comes during May, and if you are fond of the fruit, they are well worth freezing, as the season is relatively short.

*Serves 6*

*Pastry:*
150 g (5 oz) plain flour, sifted
75 g (3 oz) butter, cut into small chunks
50 g (2 oz) caster sugar
2 egg yolks
*Filling:*
225 g (8 oz) gooseberries, topped and tailed
75 g (3 oz) sugar
4 tablespoons water
*Glaze:*
4 tablespoons apricot jam, sieved
2 tablespoons water
1 × 150 ml (¼ pint) carton double or whipping cream, whipped, to decorate

*Preparation time: 40 minutes, plus cooling*
*Cooking time: 45 minutes*
*Oven: 180°C, 350°F, Gas Mark 4;*
*then: 150°C, 300°F, Gas Mark 2*

1. Place the flour on a board or marble slab, and make a well in the centre. Put the butter, caster sugar and yolks into the well, then gradually work all the ingredients together until they form a stiff dough. Knead gently until smooth.
2. To make the boats, roll out the pastry and use it to line 12 boat-shaped pastry moulds.
3. Prick the bases of the pastry and bake in a preheated oven for 8-10 minutes, or until the pastry is crisp, and golden brown around the edges. Remove the pastry boats from the tins, and allow them to cool on a wire tray.
4. Place the gooseberries in an ovenproof dish, sprinkle with the sugar, then pour over the water. Cook in a preheated cool oven until the fruit is just tender. The cooking time depends on the ripeness of the gooseberries, but remove them from the oven before they begin to break up. Allow to cool in the dish.
5. When the gooseberries are quite cold, fill them into the pastry boats and prepare the glaze.
6. Place the apricot jam and water in a small saucepan and allow to melt over a gentle heat. Bring to simmering point and cook for 2-3 minutes. Using a pastry brush, glaze each pastry boat.
7. For the decoration, fill the whipped cream into a forcing bag fitted with a small rose tube, and pipe each boat with a shell pattern.

*Glazed gooseberry boats*

# TWO FRUITS COMPOTE

300 ml (½ pint) unsweetened orange juice
4 tablespoons lemon juice
2 tablespoons apricot jam
3 firm pears, peeled, halved, cored and cut
into sections
8 apricots, blanched and skinned
twists of orange peel, to decorate (optional)

*Preparation time: 10-15 minutes*
*Cooking time: about 20 minutes*

1. Put the orange juice, lemon juice and apricot jam into a pan; stir over a gentle heat until the jam has dissolved.
2. Add the prepared fruits to the syrup; cover the pan, bring to the boil and simmer gently for about 12-15 minutes, until the pears are tender. Cool slightly.
3. Spoon into one large or 4 small dishes (heatproof ones if the compote is very hot), and decorate with a twist of orange peel if liked.

# GRAPE AND WHITE WINE JELLY

4 teaspoons powdered gelatine
300 ml (½ pint) apple juice
300 ml (½ pint) dry white wine
225 g (8 oz) green grapes, skinned, halved and
seeded
clusters of green grapes, to decorate

*Preparation time: about 25 minutes, plus chilling*

1. Place the gelatine and 3 tablespoons of the apple juice in a small bowl. Stand in a saucepan of hot water and stir over a gentle heat until dissolved. Combine with the remaining apple juice and white wine and put to one side until syrupy.
2. Lightly oil one 900 ml (1½ pint) mould, or 4 small ones.
3. Stir the prepared grapes into the syrupy jelly and pour into the mould.
4. Chill for about 2-3 hours, until set.
5. Carefully turn out the jelly on to a serving plate and decorate with small clusters of grapes.

# APPLE LIME CRUNCH

450 g (1 lb) cooking apples, peeled, cored and
sliced
2 tablespoons freshly squeezed lime juice
2 tablespoons water
sugar to taste
1 egg, separated
4 tablespoons muesli, lightly toasted
4 teaspoons lime curd or lime marmalade
4 thin slices of lime, to decorate

*Preparation time: 20-25 minutes, plus chilling*
*Cooking time: about 5 minutes*

1. Put the apples into a pan with the lime juice and water; cover and simmer gently until the apples are soft and pulpy. Add sugar to taste. Chill.
2. Beat the egg yolk into the cooked apple; whisk the egg white until stiff but not dry, and fold lightly but thoroughly into the apple mixture.
3. Put half the apple mixture into 4 tall glasses, and sprinkle the toasted muesli over the top. Add a spoonful of lime curd or lime marmalade and top up with the remaining apple mixture.
4. Decorate each one with a twisted lime slice, and serve immediately.

FROM THE RIGHT: *Apple lime crunch; Grape and white wine jelly; Two fruits compote*

# GOOSEBERRY JELLY

450 g (1 lb) gooseberries, topped and tailed
150 ml (¼ pint) water
300 ml (½ pint) pure apple juice
sugar to taste
4 teaspoons powdered gelatine
3 tablespoons dry white wine
fresh angelica leaves or fresh gooseberries,
to decorate

*Preparation time: 20 minutes, plus chilling*
*Cooking time: 6-8 minutes*

1. Lightly oil a 900 ml (1½ pint) mould.
2. Put the gooseberries into a pan with the water and simmer until soft and pulpy. Blend the fruit in a food processor until smooth.
3. Mix the purée with apple juice and sugar to taste.
4. Dissolve the gelatine in the white wine and add to the gooseberry mixture; mix thoroughly and pour into the prepared mould. Chill for 2-3 hours until set.
5. Carefully unmould the set jelly on to a serving plate, and decorate with angelica leaves or fresh gooseberries.

# WHOLE STRAWBERRY ICE CREAM

3 egg yolks
1 tablespoon redcurrant jelly
1 tablespoon red vermouth
300 ml (½ pint) plain unsweetened yogurt
350 g (12 oz) ripe strawberries, hulled
4-6 strawberries with stalks, halved, to decorate

*Preparation time: 25 minutes, plus freezing*

1. Put the egg yolks into a food processor with the redcurrant jelly, vermouth, yogurt, and half the strawberries; blend until smooth.
2. Transfer the mixture to a shallow container, and freeze until it starts to harden around the edges.
3. Tip the ice cream into a bowl and beat to break up the ice crystals. Chop the remaining strawberries and mix into the semi-set ice cream. Return to the container and freeze until quite firm.
4. Scoop the ice cream into stemmed glasses and decorate each one with strawberry halves.

# APPLE GÂTEAU

1 sachet powdered gelatine
2 tablespoons water
450 g (1 lb) cooking apples, peeled, cored and sliced
juice and grated rind of ½ lemon
sugar to taste
1 egg yolk
4 tablespoons muesli cereal
25 g (1 oz) butter or margarine
2 dessert apples, cored and sliced
150 ml (¼ pint) apple juice

*Preparation time: 30-40 minutes, plus chilling*
*Cooking time: 20 minutes*
*Oven: 190°C, 375°F, Gas Mark 5*

1. Put half the gelatine and the water in a heatproof bowl and stir over hot water until dissolved.
2. Heat the cooking apples with the lemon rind and juice and a few tablespoons of water until tender. Add sugar to taste and beat in the egg yolk. Stir in the dissolved gelatine.
3. Bake the muesli in a preheated oven for 8 minutes. Mix with the butter or margarine while still hot.
4. Spread muesli over base of a loose-bottomed 18 cm (7 inch) cake tin. Chill for 30 minutes.
5. Poach the dessert apple slices gently in the apple juice for about 3 minutes; remove carefully and drain on paper towels.
6. Combine the remaining gelatine with 2 tablespoons of apple juice in a heatproof bowl; stir over hot water to dissolve. Stir in remaining apple juice.
7. Spread the apple purée over the muesli base; arrange the apple slices on top. Spoon over the apple juice glaze.
8. Chill for 4 hours.

CLOCKWISE FROM RIGHT: *Gooseberry jelly; Whole strawberry ice cream; Apple gâteau*

# BLACKCURRANT SESAME CRUMBLE

*Serves 4-6*

225 g (8 oz) cooking apples, peeled, cored and
thinly sliced
350 g (12 oz) blackcurrants, stripped from stalks
2 tablespoons water
40 g (1½ oz) soft light brown sugar
*Topping:*
150 g (5 oz) wholewheat flour
75 g (3 oz) hard margarine
25 g (1 oz) toasted sesame seeds
40 g (1½ oz) demerara sugar
1 teaspoon ground cinnamon
plain unsweetened yogurt or soured cream, to serve

*Preparation time: 20 minutes*
*Cooking time: 50 minutes*
*Oven: 160°C, 325°F, Gas Mark 3*

1. Simmer the apples and blackcurrants with the
water for 5 minutes. Stir in the sugar. Turn the
mixture into a shallow baking dish.
2. Rub together the flour and margarine until the
mixture is like fine crumbs, then stir in the sesame
seeds, sugar and cinnamon.
3. Sprinkle the topping over the fruit and level the
top. F
4. Stand the dish on a baking sheet. Bake in a preheated oven for 40-45 minutes, or until the topping is golden brown. Serve hot or warm.

F You can freeze the uncooked pudding for up to 2
months. Bake it from frozen, in the oven at 190°C,
375°F, Gas Mark 5 for 45-50 minutes.

# APPLE SORBET

150 ml (¼ pint) dry white wine
50 g (2 oz) soft light brown sugar
a strip of thinly-pared lemon rind
2 tablespoons lemon juice
a piece of fresh root ginger, peeled
450 g (1 lb) cooking apples, peeled, cored and sliced
small angelica or other herb leaves, to decorate

*Preparation time: 15 minutes, plus 4-5 hours freezing*
*Cooking time: 15 minutes*

1. Put the wine, sugar, lemon rind, lemon juice and
ginger into a pan and stir over a low heat until the
sugar has dissolved. Increase the heat and bring to
the boil.

CLOCKWISE FROM THE LEFT: *Apple sorbet; Blackcurrant
sesame crumble; Greengage brandy snap cups*

2. Add the apple slices and poach them for 8-10 minutes, or until they are tender. Remove from the heat and leave to cool.
3. Discard the lemon rind and ginger and liquidize the fruit and juice in a blender.
4. Pour the mixture into a container, cover with foil and freeze for 1 hour.
5. Turn the mixture into a chilled bowl and beat it to break down the ice crystals.
6. Return the mixture to the freezer for 3-4 hours, until it is firm. F
7. To serve, transfer the sorbet to the refrigerator for about 30 minutes. Serve it in scoops, decorated with the herb leaves.

F You can store the sorbet for up to 2 months without loss of flavour.

# GREENGAGE BRANDY SNAP CUPS

*Serves 6*

50 g (2 oz) wholewheat flour
½ teaspoon ground ginger
50 g (2 oz) soft light brown sugar
2 tablespoons clear honey
50 g (2 oz) soft margarine
½ teaspoon lemon rind
1 teaspoon lemon juice
*Filling:*
450 g (1 lb) greengages, stoned
2 tablespoons water
3 tablespoons clear honey
300 ml (½ pint) plain unsweetened yogurt
scented geranium leaves, to decorate
1 orange, for making the cups

*Preparation time: 45 minutes, plus cooling*
*Cooking time: 40 minutes*
*Oven: 190°C, 375°F, Gas Mark 5*

1. Mix together the flour and ginger. Heat the sugar, honey and margarine over a low heat and stir together until the ingredients are well blended. Remove the pan from the heat, tip in the flour and beat well. Beat in the lemon rind and lemon juice.
2. Line a baking tray with non-stick silicone paper. Drop teaspoonfuls of the mixture on to the baking tray, leaving plenty of space between them.
3. Bake in a preheated oven for 8-10 minutes. Remove the brandy snaps one at a time and – working very quickly, before they harden – press each one over an orange held in the palm of your hand to form the cups. Place the brandy snap cups upside down on a wire rack to cool. When they are completely cold, they can be stored in an airtight tin for up to 10 days.
4. To make the filling, reserve 3 greengages to decorate and simmer the remainder in the water and honey syrup. When the greengages are soft, press them through a sieve. Return the purée to the pan and simmer until it is thick. Set aside to cool.
5. Beat together the cooled purée and the yogurt.
6. Just before serving, fill the cups with the purée. Cut the reserved greengages into thin slices and arrange a few on each cup to form a flower shape. Arrange scented geranium leaves in the centre to decorate.

# PEARS WITH FRESH RASPBERRY SAUCE

4 large firm pears
300 ml (½ pint) orange juice
bay leaf
small piece of cinnamon stick
1 tablespoon clear honey
225 g (8 oz) fresh raspberries

*Preparation time: about 20 minutes, plus cooling*
*Cooking time: 10 minutes*

1. Peel, halve and core the pears. Place them in a saucepan with the orange juice, bay leaf, cinnamon stick and honey. Cover the pan and simmer gently for 10 minutes.
2. Turn the pear halves over in their cooking liquid; cover the pan and leave them to cool in their liquid.
3. Blend the raspberries in the liquidizer until smooth; add sufficient of the pear cooking liquid to give a thin coating consistency.
4. Arrange the drained pear halves in a shallow serving dish and trickle over the prepared sauce.

**Variation:**
Spoon the raspberry sauce on to individual serving plates; trickle a little plain unsweetened yogurt on top, and arrange the pear halves carefully on top.

# BLUSHING PLUMS

200 ml (⅓ pint) red wine
1 tablespoon clear honey
juice of 1 orange
100 g (4 oz) redcurrants, trimmed
12 really ripe plums, halved and stoned
sprigs of fresh lemon verbena or fresh plum leaves,
to decorate

*Preparation time: 15-20 minutes*
*Cooking time: 5 minutes*

1. Put the red wine, honey, orange juice and redcurrants into a pan; simmer for 5 minutes. Blend in the liquidizer until smooth, then strain.
2. Arrange the plum halves in a shallow dish, and decorate the rim with lemon verbena or plum leaves. Spoon over the redcurrant sauce.

# BLACKCURRANT CREAM

350 g (12 oz) fresh blackcurrants, trimmed
2 tablespoons clear honey
1 tablespoon brandy
2 egg yolks
1 teaspoon powdered gelatine
1 tablespoon water
200 ml (⅓ pint) plain unsweetened yogurt
borage flowers or small clusters of fresh
blackcurrants, to decorate

*Preparation time: 20 minutes, plus chilling*
*Cooking time: 8 minutes*

1. Put the blackcurrants into a pan with the honey and brandy; simmer gently for 8 minutes until the fruit is soft. Allow to cool.
2. Purée the cooked blackcurrants in the liquidizer until smooth; blend in the egg yolks.
3. Dissolve the gelatine in the water; beat into the blackcurrant mixture, together with the yogurt.
4. Spoon into dishes or stemmed glasses and chill for 1-2 hours until set.
5. Decorate each dessert with borage flowers or a cluster of fresh blackcurrants.

CLOCKWISE FROM TOP: *Blushing plums; Blackcurrant cream; Pears with fresh raspberry sauce*

## DAMSON FOOL WITH MACAROONS

*Serves 4-6*

750 g (1½ lb) damsons
175 g (6 oz) sugar, or to taste
½ teaspoon lemon juice
450 ml (¾ pint) double or whipping cream, whipped
2 egg whites, stiffly beaten
*Macaroons:*
2 egg whites, stiffly beaten
100 g (4 oz) caster sugar
75 g (3 oz) ground almonds
1 teaspoon vanilla essence
rice paper

*Preparation time: 1 hour, plus cooling*
*Cooking time: 40 minutes*
*Oven: 160°C, 325°F, Gas Mark 3*

1. First make the macaroons by putting the stiffly beaten egg whites in a bowl, then adding the sugar, almonds and vanilla essence and folding them in thoroughly.
2. Lay the rice paper on a baking sheet and pipe or spoon the mixture on to it in mounds about 2.5 cm (1 inch) across.
3. Put into the centre of a preheated oven and bake for 20-30 minutes, until they are set and golden brown.
4. Lift the macaroons off when cooked and cool on a wire tray.
5. Put the damsons into a saucepan with the sugar and lemon and enough water just to cover. Simmer until soft. Leave until they are cool enough, then lift them out and remove the stones. Blend the fruit in the liquidizer and turn into a large bowl.
6. Fold two-thirds of the whipped cream and all the egg white lightly but thoroughly into the damsons, seeing that you get right down to the bottom and that the mixture is an even colour.
7. Transfer the mixture to a serving bowl, decorate the top with the almond macaroons, and dot all over with the remaining whipped cream.

**Variation:**
Gooseberries can be made into a fool the same way as the damsons. The macaroons are optional.

## SUMMER PUDDING

A wonderful pudding to make in the height of summer when the garden is burgeoning with soft fruit.

*Serves 6*

10 slices of crustless white bread, not too fresh
3 tablespoons milk
750 g (1½ lb) mixed soft fruit (raspberries, redcurrants or white currants, strawberries and cherries if available)
100 g (4 oz) caster sugar
a little fresh fruit to decorate (optional)
single cream, to serve

*Preparation time: 40 minutes, plus overnight pressing*
*Cooking time: 5 minutes*

1. Lightly butter a pudding basin of 1 litre (1¾ pint) capacity.
2. Moisten the bread with the milk
3. Hull, stone, or top and tail the fruit as necessary. Cook it all very gently with the sugar for 4-5 minutes until the sugar melts and the juices run. Spoon off a few spoonfuls of juice as it cools and reserve.
4. Line the sides and bottom of the basin with the bread slices, cutting where necessary and checking there are no spaces. Reserve enough bread slices for the lid.
5. Pour in the fruit, which should come almost to the top. Cover closely with the remaining bread.
6. Put a small plate over the top (it should just fit inside the rim of the basin), and weight it with something heavy. Leave to press overnight in a cool place.
7. To serve, remove the weight and the plate. Place a serving plate over the top and reverse quickly so the pudding comes out easily in one piece.
8. Pour the remaining juices slowly all over the pudding, especially over those places where the juices might not have seeped through thoroughly.
9. Keep cold until ready to serve. Decorate with a few pieces of fresh fruit, if liked and serve with single cream.

FROM THE TOP: *Damson fool with macaroons; Summer pudding*

# PEARS POACHED IN LEMON JUICE AND WHITE WINE

When picking or buying pears for this dish, choose pears of the same size and shape, as this makes the presentation of the dish so much better. It is easier if you core the pears before peeling them. Use an apple corer or a sharp, thin-bladed knife and remove the core from the bottom of the pear. Leave the stalk to decorate if wished.

rind and juice of 2 lemons
150 ml (¼ pint) white wine
150 ml (¼ pint) water
75 g (3 oz) caster sugar
4 firm pears, cored and peeled
2 teaspoons arrowroot

*Preparation time: 20 minutes, plus cooling*
*Cooking time: 35 minutes*

1. Put the lemon rind and juice into a saucepan with the white wine, water and sugar. Bring to the boil, stirring frequently, until the sugar has dissolved.
2. Put the pears into the pan and poach for about 30 minutes until they are tender, turning carefully from time to time. Remove from the heat and leave the pears in the pan to cool in the juice.
3. When quite cold, stand the pears in a serving dish. Mix the arrowroot with a little of the juice, pour back into the pan, bring to the boil, then cook for 2-3 minutes. Leave to cool, then strain over the pears.

*Pears poached in lemon juice and white wine*

*Almond and fig baked apples*

# ALMOND AND FIG BAKED APPLES

This easily prepared dessert relies on the delicious flavour of Bramley cooking apples.

6 Bramley cooking apples
50 g (2 oz) butter
400 g (14 oz) dried figs, chopped
6 tablespoons ground almonds
3 tablespoons sherry
cream or custard, to serve

*Preparation time: 15 minutes*
*Cooking time: 35 minutes*
*Oven: 180°C, 350°F, Gas Mark 4*

1. Wash and dry the apples and remove the cores. Make a circular cut around the waist of each apple. Place in a roasting tin.
2. Melt half the butter in a small saucepan and add the figs, the almonds and the sherry. Stir over a high heat for 5 minutes.
3. Fill the apples with this mixture and top each one with a little of the remaining butter.
4. Cook in a preheated oven for 25-30 minutes, depending on the size of the apple.
5. Serve with cream or custard.

# SOMERSET STRAWBERRY SHORTCAKE

*Serves 4-6*

175 g (6 oz) plain flour, sifted
pinch of salt
100 g (4 oz) butter
1 egg, separated
75 g (3 oz) ground almonds
75 g (3 oz) caster sugar
300 ml (½ pint) double or whipping cream
1 tablespoon sugar
225 g (8 oz) strawberries, hulled

*Preparation time: 25 minutes, plus cooling*
*Cooking time: 30 minutes*
*Oven: 160°C, 325°F, Gas Mark 3*

1. Sift the flour and salt and rub in the butter.
2. Add the egg yolk, almonds and sugar and mix well.
3. Divide this mixture between 2 × 15 cm (6 inch) greased and lined sandwich tins. Prick the top slightly and bake in a preheated oven for about 30 minutes, or until it starts to shrink away from the sides. Turn out on to a wire rack to cool.
4. About 2 hours before you want to serve the shortcake, whip the cream and sugar to taste. Whip the egg white and add it to the cream.
5. Cut half the strawberries into halves or quarters and mix with half the whipped cream.
6. Spread the strawberries and cream mixture on to 1 shortcake. Place the other one on top to form a sandwich.
7. Just before serving, decorate with the rest of the strawberries and the whipped cream.

# CORNISH BURNT CREAM

*Serves 6*

6 egg yolks, beaten
1 level tablespoon caster sugar
600 ml (1 pint) double or whipping cream
1 vanilla pod
3 tablespoons caster sugar for topping

*Preparation time: 25 minutes, plus cooling overnight*
*Cooking time: 10-15 minutes*

1. Mix the beaten egg yolks with the tablespoon of sugar.
2. Put the cream with the vanilla pod in the top of a double saucepan.
3. Bring to scalding point, but do not let it boil. Lift out the vanilla pod with kitchen tongs and pour the hot cream at once on to the egg yolks, whisking continually until they are well amalgamated.
4. Put the mixture back over a gentle heat, stirring continuously until it thickens slightly, so that it runs off the whisk in ribbons. On no account let it boil.
5. Strain into a shallow flameproof dish and leave undisturbed, covered, in a cool place for 6-8 hours, or overnight.
6. Two or three hours before serving, dust the top evenly with the caster sugar, but do not let it become too thick.
7. Put under a preheated grill and, watching it all the time, colour the cream evenly, turning the dish round if necessary until the sugar melts to a golden colour.
8. Remove from the heat and leave in a cool place until ready to serve.

# DORSET APPLE CAKE

*Serves 6*

225 g (8 oz) self-raising flour
pinch of salt
pinch of mixed spice
100 g (4 oz) butter or margarine
100 g (4 oz) soft brown sugar
350 g (12 oz) cooking apples, peeled, cored and finely chopped
1½-2½ tablespoons milk
butter, to serve

*Preparation time: 20 minutes*
*Cooking time: 45 minutes-1 hour*
*Oven: 180°C, 350°F, Gas Mark 4*

1. Sift the flour, salt and mixed spice into a bowl and rub in the fat.
2. Mix the sugar with the apples and stir into the flour mixture, adding enough milk to form a soft but not sticky dough.

3. Press the dough into a 23 cm (9 inch) flan case placed on a baking sheet.
4. Bake in a preheated oven for about 45-60 minutes or until it is firm when pressed.
5. Serve while still hot and spread with butter on top.

FROM THE TOP: *Dorset apple cake; Cornish burnt cream; Somerset strawberry shortcake*

# PEACH GRANITA

350 g (12 oz) fresh ripe peaches
150 ml (¼ pint) dry white wine
150 ml (¼ pint) fresh orange juice
2 egg whites

*Preparation time: 20-25 minutes, plus freezing*
*Cooking time: 5 minutes*

1. Nick the stalk end of each peach; plunge into a bowl of boiling water for 45 seconds, then slide off the skins. Halve the fruit, removing the stones, and chop the flesh roughly.

2. Put the peach flesh into a pan with the white wine and orange juice. (If you have a very sweet tooth, add a little sugar.) Simmer gently for 5 minutes.

3. Blend the peaches and the liquid in the liquidizer until smooth. Cool.

4. Put into a shallow container; freeze until the granita is 'slushy' around the edges, then tip into a bowl and break up the ice crystals.

5. Whisk the egg whites until stiff but not dry; fold lightly but thoroughly into the partly-frozen granita. Return to container and freeze until firm.

FROM THE LEFT: *Marinated nectarines; Peach granita; Strawberry and orange chiffon*

# MARINATED NECTARINES

4 large ripe nectarines
1 lemon
1 large orange
200 ml (⅓ pint) water
4 tablespoons dry vermouth

*Preparation time: 25-30 minutes, plus chilling*

1. Nick the stalk end of each nectarine; plunge into a bowl of boiling water for 45 seconds, then slide off the skins.
2. Pare the skin from the lemon and cut into matchstick strips. Squeeze the lemon juice into a large bowl and fill up with iced water. Put the prepared nectarines into the lemon water.
3. Peel the orange thinly, removing all the pith; chop the flesh into pieces, discarding any pips. Cut the orange peel into matchstick strips.
4. Put the orange flesh into the liquidizer with the water and vermouth; blend until smooth.
5. Lift the nectarines out of the lemon water and drain.
6. Put the nectarines into a shallow dish and spoon over the prepared orange and vermouth sauce. Cover and chill for 2 hours. (No longer, otherwise the nectarines are likely to discolour.)
7. Sprinkle with the strips of lemon and orange peel and serve immediately.

# STRAWBERRY AND ORANGE CHIFFON

350 g (12 oz) ripe strawberries, hulled
6 tablespoons orange juice
finely grated rind of ½ orange
1 tablespoon honey
2 eggs, separated
2 teaspoons powdered gelatine
2 tablespoons water
4 tablespoons plain unsweetened yogurt

*Preparation time: about 40 minutes, plus chilling*

1. Reserve 4 whole strawberries for decoration.
2. Put the remaining strawberries into the liquidizer and blend until smooth.
3. Put the orange juice and rind, honey and egg yolks into a bowl; whisk until thick, light and creamy.
4. Put the gelatine and the water in a heatproof bowl and stand in a saucepan of hot water. Stir until the gelatine has dissolved.
5. Combine the strawberry purée and whisked egg yolk mixture, then stir in the dissolved gelatine and the yogurt.
6. Whisk the egg whites until stiff but not dry; as soon as the strawberry mixture is on the point of setting, fold in the whites lightly but thoroughly.
7. Spoon into glass dessert dishes and chill for 2-3 hours.
8. Decorate each dessert with one of the reserved whole strawberries and serve.

CHAPTER SIX

# COUNTRY TEAS

The country kitchen would not be complete without
the irresistible and mouthwatering aromas of a baking
day. Featuring many traditional recipes from around
the country, here is a variety of scones, breads and
teabreads, as well as a tempting selection of cakes
ranging from wholefood confections, using unusual
ingredients such as carrot and carob, to richly-filled,
classic fruit cakes. Shortbread, buns and biscuits fill
the gaps in between to provide an abundant teatime
spread.

# SPICED YEAST BUNS

*Makes 24*

450 g (1 lb) plain flour
½ teaspoon salt
1 teaspoon ground cinnamon
75 g (3 oz) lard, cut into chunks
1 tablespoon sugar
10 g (¼ oz) dried yeast
275 ml (9 fl oz) tepid milk
2 eggs, beaten
*Glaze:*
1 tablespoon water
1 tablespoon caster sugar
extra sugar, for dredging

*Preparation time: 20 minutes, plus rising*
*Cooking time: 10-15 minutes*
*Oven: 220°C, 425°F, Gas Mark 7*

1. Warm a large mixing bowl and sift in the flour, salt and cinnamon.
2. Rub in the lard until the mixture resembles fine breadcrumbs, then stir in the sugar.
3. Cream the yeast with a little of the warm milk, then return this mixture to the remaining milk. Add the beaten eggs to the milk and mix together well.
4. Make a well in the centre of the flour, and add the milk mixture, incorporating it slowly until a dough is formed.
5. Turn on to a floured board and knead for 10 minutes, then return to the mixing bowl, cover with a clean teatowel and put in a warm place to rise until the dough has doubled in bulk.
6. Knock back the dough and divide into 24 pieces. Shape each piece into a sausage about 9 cm (3½ inches) in length and 2.5 cm (1 inch) in diameter.
7. Place the buns on a baking sheet fairly close together, so that they join up during cooking.
8. Prove in a warm place for 15 minutes, then bake in a preheated oven for 10-15 minutes.
9. While the buns are cooking, place the water and sugar in a small pan, and boil together until a light syrup is formed.
10. As soon as the buns are cooked, brush them with the syrup, then dredge with caster sugar. Serve with Rhubarb and Ginger Jam (see page 123).

**Variation:**
If using fresh yeast to make this recipe, weigh out 15 g (½ oz) and place it in a small mixing bowl. Add 1 teaspoon of sugar and mix well together with a small spoon. The mixture will become runny, which means that the yeast is alive and ready to use.

*Spiced yeast buns; Almond scones*

# ALMOND SCONES

You can make a real Devon tea by spreading the scones with butter, then strawberry jam, and topping with clotted or lightly whipped double cream.

*Makes 10*

175 g (6 oz) plain flour
¼ teaspoon salt
2 teaspoons baking powder
2 tablespoons ground almonds
50 g (2 oz) butter, cut into chunks
50 g (2 oz) sultanas
120 ml (4 fl oz) milk
few drops almond essence
milk, to glaze

*Preparation time: 15 minutes*
*Cooking time: 10 minutes*
*Oven: 200°C, 400°F, Gas Mark 6*

1. Sift the flour, salt and baking powder together in a bowl, then stir in the ground almonds.
2. Add the butter and rub it in until the mixture resembles fine breadcrumbs, then stir in the sultanas.
3. Make a well in the centre of the mixture, and pour in the milk and almond essence. Mix lightly with a wooden spoon or fork until a soft dough is formed.
4. Turn the dough on to a floured board and knead gently until smooth. Roll out the dough to 1 cm (½ inch) thick and cut into rounds with a 5 cm (2 inch) cutter.
5. Place the scones on a lightly greased baking sheet, and brush the tops gently with milk.
6. Bake in a preheated oven for 7-10 minutes, or until the scones are well risen and golden brown. Remove from the oven and cool on a wire tray.

# CHERRY AND GINGER SHORTBREADS

*Makes 8-12*

25 g (1 oz) crystallized ginger
25 g (1 oz) glacé cherries
100 g (4 oz) self-raising flour
75 g (3 oz) butter or margarine
50 g (2 oz) caster sugar

*Preparation time: 30 minutes*
*Cooking time: 15 minutes*
*Oven: 160°C, 325°F, Gas Mark 3*

1. Cut the ginger and cherries into small pieces. Sift the flour and mix with the ginger and cherries. Cream the butter or margarine and sugar until soft, add the flour mixture, work together with your fingers.
2. Form into 12 to 14 medium balls, or 16 to 18 small ones. Place on lightly greased baking sheets and bake in a preheated oven for 15 minutes.

# MOIST ALMOND SLICES

*Makes 8-12*

175 (6 oz) plain flour
pinch of salt
85 g (3 oz) margarine
3 tablespoons raspberry jam
*Filling:*
225 g (8 oz) margarine
225 g (8 oz) caster sugar
50 g (2 oz) ground almonds
175 g (6 oz) ground rice
1 to 2 teaspoons almond essence
2 eggs
blanched almonds

*Preparation time: 25 minutes*
*Cooking time: 35-40 minutes*
*Oven: 190-200°C, 375-400°F, Gas Mark 5-6*

1. Sift the flour and salt into a bowl. Rub in the margarine. Add enough cold water to bind. Roll out the pastry and line a Swiss roll tin measuring 28 × 20 cm (11 × 8 inches). Spread with raspberry jam.
2. To make the filling, melt the margarine in a saucepan. Remove from the heat and beat in caster sugar, ground almonds and ground rice. Add the almond essence and eggs. Beat well and pour over the pastry. Top with blanched almonds.
3. Bake in the centre of a preheated oven for 35 to 40 minutes. Lower the heat slightly after 25 minutes, if the cake is becoming too brown. Cut into slices when hot. Allow to cool in the tin.

*Cherry and ginger shortbreads* and *moist almond slices* illustrated on page 104

# BANANA AND YOGURT TEABREAD

*Makes 1 'barrel' loaf or 1 small loaf, just under 450 g (1 lb)*

50 g (2 oz) soft margarine
90 g (3½ oz) soft light brown sugar
1 egg, beaten
100 g (4 oz) wholewheat flour
salt
1 large banana, about 150 g (5 oz), peeled
2 tablespoons plain unsweetened yogurt
50 g (2 oz) sultanas
2 tablespoons sunflower seeds

*Preparation time: 20 minutes*
*Cooking time: 1¼ hours*
*Oven: 160°C, 325°F, Gas Mark 3*

1. Grease and flour a cleaned 825 g (29 oz) food can with the top removed or a 20 × 10 cm (8 × 4 inch) loaf tin.
2. Cream the margarine and sugar together until they are light and fluffy, then beat in the egg.
3. Sift the flour and salt and tip in any bran left in the sieve. Mash the banana with the yogurt.
4. Add the flour mixture and the banana alternately to the creamed fat, beating well between each addition. Stir in the sultanas and sunflower seeds.
5. Spoon the mixture into the prepared can or loaf tin. Bake in a preheated oven for 1-1¼ hours, until the loaf is cooked. Test it by piercing the centre with a fine skewer.

# AYRSHIRE PAN SCONES

*Makes 12 wedges*
225 g (8 oz) strong wholewheat flour
1 teaspoon bicarbonate of soda
1 teaspoon salt
1 teaspoon cream of tartar
25 g (1 oz) soft margarine
15 g (½ oz) soft light brown sugar
150 ml (¼ pint) plain unsweetened yogurt
100 ml (3½ fl oz) soured cream
oil, for brushing

*Preparation time: 20 minutes*
*Cooking time: 30 minutes*

CLOCKWISE FROM THE TOP: *Banana and yogurt teabread; Herb scones; Ayrshire pan scones*

1. Sift the flour, soda, salt and cream of tartar and tip in any bran remaining in the sieve. Rub in the margarine and stir in the sugar. Stir in the yogurt and soured cream. Shape the mixture into a dough and knead it lightly. [A]
2. Divide the dough into 2 equal pieces and shape each one to a round. Flatten the pieces until they are 2 cm (¾ inch) thick.
3. Heat a heavy-based frying pan and very lightly brush it with oil.
4. Cook each scone over moderate heat for 6-7 minutes, until it is well browned on the underside. Flip it over and cook the other side. Transfer the

# HERB SCONES

*Makes 8-10 scones*

225 g (8 oz) wholewheat flour
½ teaspoon bicarbonate of soda
½ teaspoon salt
40 g (1½ oz) white vegetable fat
1 teaspoon dried oregano
½ teaspoon dried basil
75 g (3 oz) Gouda cheese, grated
150 ml (¼ pint) buttermilk
1 tablespoon tomato purée
milk, for brushing

*Preparation time: 15 minutes*
*Cooking time: 20 minutes*
*Oven: 200°C, 400°F, Gas Mark 6*

If you cannot obtain buttermilk – which, like yogurt, gives the necessary acid and the characteristic flavour to scones of all kinds – you can substitute milk soured with lemon juice. Stir in teaspoon lemon juice to each 300 ml (1 pint) milk.

1. Sift the flour, soda and salt and tip in any bran left in the sieve. Rub in the fat until the mixture is like fine breadcrumbs. Stir in the dried herbs and half the cheese. Gradually stir the milk into the tomato purée so that it is well blended. Pour the mixture on to the dry ingredients and mix to form a firm dough.
2. Roll out the dough on a lightly-floured board to a thickness of about 2 cm (¾ inch).
3. Using a 5 cm (2 inch) cutter, cut out rounds of the dough. Gather up the pieces into a ball, roll them out again and cut more rounds.
4. Place the scone rounds on a baking sheet and sprinkle them with the remaining cheese.
5. Bake in a preheated oven for 20 minutes, or until the scones are well risen and springy to the touch.
6. Transfer them to a wire rack to cool.

scone to a wire rack to cool. Cook the remaining dough in the same way. ☐F☐
5. Serve cut into wedges with honey and low fat soft cheese.

☐A☐ These scones do not stay fresh for more than 1 day, but the dough can be made in advance, wrapped in foil and stored in the refrigerator overnight. Leave it to relax at room temperature for about 30 minutes before cooking.
☐F☐ Freeze for up to 1 month. Thaw the scones in the oven at 180°C, 350°F, Gas Mark 4 for 10-15 minutes.

# APPLE PIE WITH ALMOND PASTRY

The pie is eaten warm with clotted cream. It can either be made in a shallow dish with a double crust, as described here, or in a deeper dish with a single crust.

*Serves 4-6*

*Pastry:*
175 g (6 oz) plain flour
2 rounded tablespoons ground almonds
100 g (4 oz) butter, warm
25 g (1 oz) icing sugar, sifted
1 egg yolk
2 tablespoons cold water
a little milk for glazing
*Filling:*
750 g (1½ lb) apples, peeled, cored and sliced, or
450 g (1 lb) apples and 225 g (½ lb) blackberries
2 teaspoons lemon juice
100 g (4 oz) caster sugar

*Preparation time: 50 minutes, plus chilling*
*Cooking time: 40 minutes*
*Oven: 200°C, 400°F, Gas Mark 6;*
*then: 160°C, 325°F, Gas Mark 3*

1. First make the pastry by putting the flour and almonds into the basin, then add the butter, at room temperature. Cut into small pieces and rub into the flour. Add the icing sugar, mixing well.
2. Make a well in the centre and put the egg yolk and water mixed together into it. Mix to a rough dough in the basin with a fork.
3. Turn on to a lightly floured surface and knead gently until it is quite smooth. Roll into a ball and chill for at least 30 minutes before using.
4. If using blackberries, put them into a dish and place in the oven while it is heating up.
5. Divide the pastry into two and roll out to fit a 20 cm (8 inch) shallow pie plate and line it with one half of the pastry. Fill the pie with the apples (or blackberries and apples), the lemon juice, about 3-4 tablespoons of blackberry juice, if using, from the warmed dish, and the sugar.
6. Dampen the edges and lay the other piece of pastry on top, pressing down the edges with finger and thumb.
7. Make a small slit in the middle to let the steam out, or prick lightly all over the top, and brush with a little milk.
8. Bake in the centre of a preheated oven for 20 minutes, then reduce the oven temperature for a further 15-20 minutes.

FROM THE LEFT: *Fairings; Apple pie with almond pastry*

*Devonshire splits*

# FAIRINGS

These are little biscuits sold at the fairs which were held all over the West Country. There are several kinds but these are the crunchy Cornish variety.

*Makes about 30*

225 g (8 oz) self-raising flour
1½ teaspoons bicarbonate of soda
pinch of salt
1 teaspoon ground ginger
1 teaspoon mixed spice
½ teaspoon ground cinnamon
100 g (4 oz) butter or margarine
50 g (2 oz) sugar
100 g (4 oz) golden syrup

*Preparation time: 25 minutes*
*Cooking time: about 10 minutes*
*Oven: 190°C, 375°F, Gas Mark 5*

1. Sift the flour, bicarbonate of soda, salt and spices together and mix well.
2. Rub in the butter or margarine and add the sugar, until the mixture looks like breadcrumbs.
3. Heat the golden syrup a little, then pour it into the paste and knead until it forms a firm dough.
4. Flour your hands and roll the mixture into small balls, then put on to a greased baking sheet, well spaced out. Flatten with the back of a spoon.
5. Cook in a preheated oven for about 10 minutes or until golden brown. Cool on a wire tray.

# DEVONSHIRE SPLITS

These yeasted buns form the basis of many 'Cream Teas' in Devon and Cornwall. They are split open and served with clotted cream and strawberry or raspberry jam. If served with clotted cream and black treacle they are known as 'Thunder and Lightning'.

*Makes about 18*

15 g (½ oz) fresh yeast or 10 g (¼ oz) dried yeast
½ teaspoon caster sugar
150 ml (¼ pint) tepid water
25 g (1 oz) lard
50 g (2 oz) butter
6 tablespoons milk
450 g (1 lb) plain flour
pinch of salt
*To serve:*
icing sugar
clotted or whipped cream
jam

*Preparation time: 15 minutes, plus rising*
*Cooking time: 20 minutes*
*Oven: 200°C, 400°F, Gas Mark 6*

1. Sprinkle the fresh yeast and sugar over the tepid water and leave until it is frothy. If using dried yeast, mix with the sugar and tepid water and leave in a warm place for about 10 minutes, until it becomes frothy.
2. Put the lard, butter and milk into a small saucepan and heat gently until the fats have melted, but on no account let it boil. Remove from the heat and allow to cool.
3. Meanwhile sift the flour and salt into a mixing bowl, make a well in the centre and pour in the yeast and milk mixtures, then mix with the fingers until it is soft but not sticky.
4. Turn on to a floured surface and knead gently for 5 minutes, then put into a bowl, cover and leave in a warm place for 1 hour.
5. Take out and knead again a little, then shape into about 18 small balls. Place them on a greased baking sheet a little apart and leave until they have spread and are just touching.
6. Bake in a preheated oven for about 20 minutes or until risen. When cooked, they should sound hollow when tapped. Dust with icing sugar, and serve with clotted cream and jam.

# DUNDEE CAKE

*Makes one 23 cm (9 inch) diameter cake*

450 g (1 lb) butter
175 g (6 oz) soft brown sugar
6 tablespoons orange juice
4 tablespoons lemon juice
grated rind of 1 orange
grated rind of 1 lemon
3 eggs, beaten
175 g (6 oz) currants
175 g (6 oz) sultanas
100 g (4 oz) raisins, chopped
100 g (4 oz) candied pineapple (optional)
100 g (4 oz) blanched almonds, coarsely chopped
50 g (2 oz) crystallized ginger, chopped (optional)
75 g (3 oz) glacé cherries, chopped
75 g (3 oz) mixed peel, chopped
450 g (1 lb) self-raising flour
*To decorate:*
12 whole, blanched almonds
milk

*Preparation time: 15 minutes*
*Cooking time: 2 hours*
*Oven: 180°C, 350°F, Gas Mark 4;*
*then: 150°C, 300°F, Gas Mark 2*

1. Line a 23 cm (9 inch) diameter cake tin with greased greaseproof paper to 1 cm (½ inch) above the top of the tin.
2. In a large mixing bowl, cream together the butter and sugar and add the juices and grated rinds of the orange and lemon. Beat in the eggs.
3. Mix together all the remaining ingredients and fold into the mixture.
4. Fill the tin not more than two-thirds full and make a deep depression in the centre.
5. Dip the whole, blanched almonds in milk and arrange them on the top of the cake. Put the cake in a preheated oven and bake for 1 hour.
6. Reduce the oven temperature and bake for another 1 hour. Cover the top with a piece of foil if it is browning too much.
7. Test with a fine skewer pushed into the centre of the cake: if the skewer comes out clean, the cake is done. Place the tin on a wire tray to cool, then turn out and cool completely on a wire tray. [A]

[A] This cake will keep in an airtight container for several weeks.

# BLACK BUN

*Serves 10-12*

Famous throughout Scotland since the eighteenth century, Black Bun was often made at Christmas, when it was sometimes called Yule Cake. The filling is much like a rich, black Christmas pudding, but the delicate envelope of pastry gives it a special character. It requires neither eggs nor sugar.

*Pastry:*
450 g (1 lb) plain flour
¼ teaspoon salt
225 g (8 oz) butter
*Filling:*
350 g (12 oz) self-raising flour
1 teaspoon ground cinnamon
¼ teaspoon freshly ground black pepper
¼ teaspoon grated nutmeg
450 g (1 lb) seedless raisins
450 g (1 lb) currants
50 g (2 oz) mixed peel (optional)
50 g (2 oz) glacé cherries, chopped
100 g (4 oz) blanched almonds, coarsely chopped
2 tablespoons whisky
milk
2 egg yolks, beaten

*Preparation time: 30 minutes, plus cooling*
*Cooking time: 2½ hours*
*Oven: 180°C, 350°F, Gas Mark 4*

1. Mix the flour and salt together and rub in the butter until you have a crumb-like consistency. Mix in 1 tablespoon of very cold water. If the dough is still crumbly, add another and stir and mix until it will come away from the bowl in one piece, leaving the bowl clean.
2. Flour a board and roll the pastry out to a little less than 5 mm (¼ inch) thickness. Grease either a 25 × 13 cm (10 × 5 inch) bread tin, or a loose-bottomed 20 cm (8 inch) cake tin. Line the bread or cake tin, moulding the pastry against the sides and making sure there are no holes. Set aside a piece for the lid.
3. Mix the flour, cinnamon, pepper and nutmeg together, then add all the fruit and the almonds. Stir well together. Add the whisky and stir in, then add enough milk to bring it to a stiff consistency.
4. Fill the tin and smooth off flat at the top. Roll out the pastry lid and lay it on loosely, so that the

inside can rise a little. Thrust a long skewer through the lid and filling, right to the bottom, in about 8 places. Lightly prick the lid all over with a fork. Brush over with the beaten egg yolks.

5. Put the tin in a preheated oven and bake for 2½

hours.

6. Allow the bun to stand in the tin on a wire tray for 30 minutes before turning out.

FROM THE LEFT: *Dundee cake; Black bun*

# SINGING HINNIES

'Hinny' is a North Country term of endearment used to children. Singing hinnies are so-called because the hinny used to be baked on an oiled griddle and its sizzling sound was thought to sound like singing. It is really a fried scone.

225 g (8 oz) plain flour, sifted
pinch of salt
50 g (2 oz) butter
50 g (2 oz) lard
50 g (2 oz) sugar (optional)
75 g (3 oz) currants
1 teaspoon baking powder
2-3 tablespoons milk or sour cream

*Preparation time: 30 minutes*
*Cooking time: 15 minutes*

1. Put the flour and salt into a bowl. Rub in the butter and lard until the mixture is like breadcrumbs.
2. Stir in the remaining dry ingredients and mix to a stiff dough with the milk or sour cream.
3. Roll into a ball, then turn out and flatten into a round cake about 1 cm (½ inch) thick.
4. Heat and lightly grease a pan or griddle. Place the hinny in the pan, prick the top all over and when brown on the bottom, turn over and do the other side.
5. Serve piping hot, cut into wedges, spread liberally with butter.

FROM THE TOP, CLOCKWISE: *Singing hinnies; Cumberland rum nicky; Preston gingerbread*

# PRESTON GINGERBREAD

This dry, crunchy gingerbread is best kept in an airtight tin for 2-3 days before eating.

*Serves about 6*

350 g (12 oz) plain flour
1 rounded teaspoon ground ginger
pinch of grated nutmeg
pinch of mixed spice
50 g (2 oz) butter, at room temperature
100 g (4 oz) black treacle
½ level teaspoon bicarbonate
of soda
3 tablespoons milk, warm
1 egg (size 1), beaten

*Preparation time: 30 minutes*
*Cooking time: 50 minutes*
*Oven: 180°C, 350°F, Gas Mark 4*

1. Grease and line a deep tin, 25 × 20 cm (10 × 8 inches).
2. Sift the flour and spices together, then rub in the butter until it is like fine breadcrumbs.
3. Warm the treacle gently. Mix the bicarbonate of soda well into the warm milk, add to the treacle and pour into the flour mixture, combining thoroughly.
4. Add the beaten egg and beat the mixture gently but thoroughly.
5. Pour into the prepared tin and bake in a preheated oven for 45 minutes or until firm when pressed.
6. Leave to cool in the tin for 5 minutes before turning out on to a wire tray.
7. Leave for a day before cutting.

# CUMBERLAND RUM NICKY

A traditional pie from Cumbria richly flavoured
with apples, dates and rum.

*Serves about 6*

100 g (4 oz) cooking dates, stoned and chopped
1 tablespoon water
350 g (12 oz) shortcrust pastry, chilled
3 medium cooking apples,
peeled, cored and sliced
1 round tablespoon demerara sugar
2 tablespoons rum
50 g (2 oz) butter
a little milk

*Preparation time: 30 minutes*
*Cooking time: 45 minutes*
*Oven: 200°C, 400°F, Gas Mark 6;*
*then: 180°C, 350°F, Gas Mark 4*

1. Put the chopped dates into a saucepan and add the water. Soften them over a low heat, then cool completely.
2. Divide the pastry in half. Roll out one half of the pastry to line a greased 17-20 cm (7-8 inch) shallow pie plate.
3. Place the sliced apples on the pastry and scatter the sugar over them.
4. Mix the rum with the butter into the dates and spread over the apples, then roll out the remaining pastry for a lid, dampening the edges and pressing them down.
5. Lightly prick over the top with a fork, brush with milk and bake in a preheated oven for 15 minutes, then reduce the oven temperature and continue cooking for a further 15 minutes or until the top is golden brown.
6. Serve cut into wedges, hot or cold, with lightly whipped cream.

# SAND CAKE

75 g (3 oz) butter or margarine
100 g (4 oz) caster sugar
2 eggs, well beaten
finely grated rind of 1 lemon
100 g (4 oz) cornflour
25 g (1 oz) plain flour
1½ teaspoons baking powder
*Icing:*
3 teaspoons lemon juice
1 teaspoon water
100 g (4 oz) icing sugar, sifted

*Preparation time: 20 minutes*
*Cooking time: 55 minutes*
*Oven: 180°C, 350°F, Gas Mark 4*

1. Cream the butter or margarine with the sugar, until light, fluffy and pale. Gradually beat in the eggs and add the lemon rind. Sift the cornflour with the flour and baking powder and fold into the mixture.
2. Turn into a well-greased 450 g (1 lb) loaf tin. Bake in a preheated oven for 50 minutes, until a skewer unserted into the centre comes out clean. Turn on to a wire tack and leave to cool.
3. To make the icing, mix the lemon juice and water into the icing sugar in a small saucepan. Stir over low heat until melted and just warm.
4. Immediately pour the icing over the cake and allow it to run down the sides. Leave to set.

# ORANGE TART

*Serves 6*

225 g (8 oz) shortcrust pastry
finely grated rind of 3 medium oranges
finely grated rind and juice of 1 lemon
400 ml (14 fl oz) orange juice
150 g (5 oz) caster sugar
3 tablespoons cornflour
5 eggs, separated

*Preparation time: 30 minutes*
*Cooking time: 1 hour*
*Oven: 200°C, 400°F, Gas Mark 6;*
*then: 150°C, 300°F, Gas Mark 2*

1. Roll out the pastry and use to line a 23 cm (9 inch) flan tin. Bake blind in a preheated oven for 15 minutes, then remove the beans and paper and bake for a further 5 minutes.
2. Mix the orange and lemon rinds and orange juice with 100 g (4 oz) sugar and the cornflour in a saucepan. Blend well and bring to the boil, stirring all the time. Lower the heat and cook for 1 minute. Remove from the heat and stir in the egg yolks and lemon juice. Pour the filling into the pastry case.
3. Lower the oven temperature. Beat the egg whites with the remaining sugar until they form stiff peaks. Pile the meringue on top, to cover the filling completely. Return to the oven and bake for 30 minutes, or until the meringue is crisp and lightly browned.

# TIPSY CAKE

*Serves 8*

1 large sponge cake or 8 small ones
3 tablespoons apricot jam
350 ml (12 fl oz) sweet sherry or madeira or marsala
3 tablespoons orange juice, strained
75 g (3 oz) caster sugar
600 ml (1 pint) double cream
225 g (8 oz) blanched almonds, split and toasted

*Preparation time: 45 minutes, plus overnight chilling*
*Cooking time: 5 minutes*
*Oven: 180°C, 350°F, Gas Mark 4*

1. Cut the cake into 8 sections and stick them back together with apricot jam, or stick the 8 small cakes together.
2. Cut out a well in the top of the cake, reserving the cut-out piece to put back later. Fill the well with wine and pour the remaining wine all over the cake.
3. Chill in the refrigerator overnight, spooning the wine over the cake from time to time. Replace the cut-out piece of cake next day.
4. Whip the orange juice, sugar and cream until soft peaks form and spoon over the cake. Arrange the almonds in a decorative pattern over the cake. Serve immediately.

FROM THE BOTTOM, CLOCKWISE: *Tipsy cake; Orange tart; Sand cake*

# APRICOT CAKE

*Makes one 18 cm (7 inch) cake*

100 g (4 oz) soft margarine
100 g (4 oz) soft light brown sugar
2 large eggs, beaten
200 g (7 oz) wholewheat self-raising flour
½ teaspoon baking powder
½ teaspoon ground cinnamon
225 g (8 oz) dried apricots, soaked, drained and chopped
100 g (4 oz) seedless raisins
2 tablespoons demerara sugar
*Topping:*
100 g (4 oz) dried apricots, soaked and drained
150 ml (¼ pint) soured cream
1 tablespoon clear honey
2 tablespoons blanched almonds, toasted and chopped

*Preparation time: 35 minutes, plus soaking*
*Cooking time: 1½ hours*
*Oven: 160°C, 325°F, Gas Mark 3*

1. Grease and line an 18 cm (7 inch) cake tin.
2. Beat the margarine and sugar together until light and fluffy, then gradually beat in the eggs. Sift the flour, baking powder and cinnamon and tip in any bran left in the sieve. Add the dry ingredients, a little at a time to the creamed mixture. Stir in the apricots and raisins and beat well.
3. Turn the mixture into the prepared cake tin, level the top and sprinkle on the demerara sugar.
4. Bake in a preheated oven for 1½ hours, or until a skewer pierced through the centre of the cake comes out clean.
5. Stand the cake in its tin on a wire rack to cool, then turn out, peel off the paper and leave the cake to become completely cool. F
6. Liquidize the apricots in a blender and beat in the soured cream and honey.
7. Spread the topping over the cake and sprinkle the chopped nuts around the edge, to decorate.

F Open-freeze the cake, then close-wrap it in foil and freeze for up to 6 months. Thaw at room temperature for 6-7 hours.

# CAROB HONEY CAKE

*Makes one 20 cm (8 inch) flat cake*

75 g (3 oz) soft light brown sugar
175 g (6 oz) clear honey
50 g (2 oz) wholewheat flour
3 tablespoons carob powder
½ teaspoon ground cinnamon
25 g (1 oz) ground almonds
1 tablespoon orange rind
50 g (2 oz) candied orange peel, chopped
175 g (6 oz) hazelnuts
100 g (4 oz) blanched almonds, lightly toasted

*Preparation time: 20 minutes*
*Cooking time: 40 minutes*
*Oven: 140°C, 275°F, Gas Mark 1*

# SPICY CARROT CAKE

*Makes one 23 cm (9 inch) cake*

2 medium bananas, peeled and mashed
150 g (5 oz) soft light brown sugar
3 eggs, beaten
275 g (10 oz) wholewheat flour
1 teaspoon bicarbonate of soda
1 teaspoon salt
2 teaspoons baking powder
1 teaspoon mixed ground spice
50 g (2 oz) walnuts, chopped
175 ml (6 fl oz) sunflower oil
175 g (6 oz) carrot, grated
*Topping:*
175 g (6 oz) low fat soft cheese
40 g (1½ oz) soft light brown sugar
1 teaspoon lemon rind
2 teaspoons lemon juice
lemon slices, quartered, to decorate

*Preparation time: 30 minutes*
*Cooking time: 1 hour 5 minutes*
*Oven: 180°C, 350°F, Gas Mark 4*

1. Grease and line a 23 cm (9 inch) round cake tin.
2. Beat the bananas and sugar until they are well blended. Gradually beat in the eggs. Sift the flour, soda, salt, baking powder and spice and tip in any bran left in the sieve. Beat into the banana mixture a little at a time with the chopped walnuts. Beat in the oil, then stir in the grated carrot. Beat well until the mixture is smooth.
3. Turn the mixture into the prepared cake tin.
4. Bake in a preheated oven for about 1 hour 5 minutes, or until the cake is 'set' and golden brown. Test by piercing it through the centre with a fine skewer, which should come out clean if the cake is done.
5. Leave the cake in the tin and place on a wire rack to cool, then turn out, peel off the paper and leave the cake to become completely cold.
6. Mix the cheese, sugar, lemon rind and juice together in a bowl.
7. Spread the mixture over the top of the cake. Arrange the lemon slices on top to decorate.

CLOCKWISE FROM THE TOP: *Carrot cake; Carob honey cake; Apricot cake*

1. Melt the sugar and honey over a low heat, then bring to simmering point and simmer, stirring frequently, for 10 minutes.
2. Sift the flour, carob powder and cinnamon, tip in any bran left in the sieve and stir in the ground almonds and orange rind. Pour on the honey mixture, stir quickly, then stir in the peel and nuts. Beat thoroughly.
3. Spread the mixture into a 20 cm (8 inch) greased and floured plain flan ring on a baking sheet or a loose-based tin.
4. Bake in a preheated oven for 30 minutes, until the cake is firm. Cool in the flan ring on a wire rack.
5. To store the cake, close-wrap it in foil once it is cold and put it in a container in the refrigerator.

# CELEBRATION CAKE

*Makes one 20 cm (8 inch) cake*

200 g (7 oz) dried stoned dates, finely chopped
150 ml (¼ pint) milk, plus extra if needed (see method)
100 g (4 oz) soft margarine
3 eggs, beaten
225 g (8 oz) wholewheat flour
2 teaspoons baking powder
1 teaspoon ground cinnamon
½ teaspoon ground ginger
a large pinch of grated nutmeg
2 teaspoons orange rind
1 tablespoon orange juice
50 g (2 oz) ground almonds
50 g (2 oz) blanched almonds, chopped
225 g (8 oz) seedless raisins
175 g (6 oz) currants
50 g (2 oz) sultanas
50 g (2 oz) candied orange peel, chopped
*Apricot paste:*
100 g (4 oz) blanched almonds
225 g (8 oz) dried apricots, chopped
2 tablespoons soft light brown sugar
1 tablespoon lemon juice
1 tablespoon clear honey, warmed

*Preparation time: 1 hour*
*Cooking time: 3¾ hours*
*Oven: 150°C, 300°F, Gas Mark 2*

1. Grease a 20 cm (8 inch) cake tin and line it with greased greaseproof paper.
2. Mash the dates with the milk and heat them over a very low heat, stirring constantly, until they form a thick paste. Set aside to cool.
3. Beat the cooled date paste with the margarine. Beat in the eggs, a little at a time.
4. Sift the flour, baking powder and spices. Add any bran left in the sieve and the orange rind.
5. Gradually add the dry ingredients to the date mixture, beating all the time. Beat in the orange juice, ground and chopped almonds, raisins, currants, sultanas and peel. Beat the mixture well and add a very little milk if necessary to give a firm dropping consistency.
6. Turn the mixture into the prepared tin and level the top.
7. Bake in a preheated oven for 2¾-3 hours, until a fine skewer pierced through the centre of the cake comes out clean.
8. Leave the cake in the tin, stand it on a wire rack to cool, then turn out. F
9. To make the apricot paste, grind the almonds until they are as fine as semolina. Reserve 2 teaspoons of the ground almonds, then add the apricots, sugar and lemon juice and process to a smooth paste. Knead the paste on a board lightly sprinkled with the remaining ground almonds. A
10. Roll out the paste to a thickness of 5 mm (¼ inch) and cut out decorative shapes, and a thick band to cover the side of the cake. Brush the side of the cake with the honey and press on the strip of apri-

cot paste. [A] Brush the decoration for the top with honey and press on to the top of the cake. Close-wrap the cake in foil and store it in an airtight tin.

[A] Your can make the apricot paste in advance, wrap it in foil and store it in an airtight container. You can also store the cut-out shapes, stacked between layers of greaseproof paper or polythene.

[F] Rewrap the cake when cold and freeze for up to 3 months. Thaw at room temperature.

FROM THE TOP: *Celebration cake; Honey spice ring*

# HONEY SPICE RING

*Makes one 1 litre (1¾ pint) ring cake*

150 g (5 oz) soft margarine
50 g (2 oz) soft light brown sugar
3 tablespoons clear honey
2 eggs, beaten
175 g (6 oz) wholewheat self-raising flour
1½ teaspoons mixed ground spice
½ teaspoon ground ginger
75 g (3 oz) walnuts, chopped
*Filling:*
225 g (8 oz) cottage cheese, sieved
150 ml (¼ pint) plain unsweetened yogurt
50 g (2 oz) soft light brown sugar
50 g (2 oz) candied orange peel, chopped
50 g (2 oz) seedless raisins
25 g (1 oz) blanched almonds, chopped
1 tablespoon orange rind
nectarine slices, to serve (optional)

*Preparation time: 1 hour, plus overnight draining*
*Cooking time: 40 minutes*
*Oven: 180°C, 350°F, Gas Mark 4*

1. Grease and flour a 1 litre (1¾ pint) ring mould.
2. Prepare the filling the day before. Beat together the cheese, yogurt and sugar. Stir in the peel, raisins, almonds and orange rind and beat well.
3. Line a sieve with a double layer of scalded muslin. Spoon in the cheese filling, cover it with muslin and put a plate and heavy weight on top. Leave the cheese to drain overnight.
4. Cream the margarine, sugar and honey together until the mixture is light and fluffy. Stir in the eggs. Sift the flour and spices and tip in any bran left in the sieve. Fold the flour into the creamed mixture and stir in the walnuts.
5. Spoon the mixture into the prepared mould.
6. Stand the mould on a baking tray and bake in a preheated oven for 40 minutes, until the cake is well risen.
7. Leave the cake to cool in the mould, then turn it out on to a wire rack until completely cold.
8. Turn the cake on to a serving dish. Fork over the cheese filling and spoon some into the centre of the ring. Decorate with nectarine slices or fresh or simmered soft fruits.

# SIMNEL CAKE

Simnel cake is a classic Easter speciality (though originally it belonged to Mid-Lent or Mothering Sunday). The 11 marzipan balls on the top of the cake represent the 12 apostles minus Judas Iscariot.

*Serves 12*

*Almond paste:*
250 g (9 oz) ground almonds
250 g (9 oz) icing sugar, sifted
3 teaspoons lemon juice
1 teaspoon orange flower water
few drops almond essence
3 egg yolks
*Cake mixture:*
200 g (7 oz) butter
200 g (7 oz) caster sugar
350 g (12 oz) plain flour
pinch of salt
1½ teaspoons baking powder
350 g (12 oz) mixed dried fruit
4 eggs, beaten
milk if required
*Decoration:*
25 g (1 oz) icing sugar
miniature Easter eggs

*Preparation time: 1 hour*
*Cooking time: 2½ hours*
*Oven: 180°C, 350°F, Gas Mark 4;*
*then: 160°C, 325°F, Gas Mark 3*

1. To make the almond paste, place the ground almonds and icing sugar in a large mixing bowl and stir well.
2. Make a well in the centre, and add the lemon juice, orange flower water, almond essence and egg yolks.
3. Gradually incorporate this mixture until if forms a dough, then turn on to a pastry board or marble slab dusted with icing sugar, and knead gently until smooth.
4. Divide the paste into 2 balls, one roughly a third of the mixture, the other two-thirds and allow them to relax in the refrigerator until needed.
5. Line a 20 cm (8 inch) loose-based cake tin with greaseproof paper and set aside.
6. Cream the butter and sugar together until light and fluffy.
7. Combine the flour, salt and baking powder, then

mix a little of the flour with the fruit, and stir to make sure the fruit is separated.
8. Beat the eggs slowly into the creamed mixture, adding a little flour from time to time if the mixture appears to be curdling, then stir in the remaining flour and fruit. Add a little milk if necessary to make a heavy dropping consistency.
9. Place half the cake mixture into the prepared tin, then roll out the smaller piece of almond paste to fit exactly over the cake mixture. Cover with the remaining cake mixture and bake in a preheated oven for 45 minutes, then reduce the heat and continue baking for another 1½-1¾ hours.
10. Allow the cake to cool in the tin, then turn on to a wire tray and leave until completely cold.
11. To decorate the cake, roll out half the remaining almond paste and trim to the exact size of the cake, and place on the top.
12. Use the remaining paste to make 11 balls of equal size and place these round the cake. Dredge the top with a little icing sugar and place under a hot grill for 2-3 minutes to allow the sugar to brown lightly.
13. When cool, place the cake on a serving dish or stand. Pile the miniature eggs in the centre or place them aound the edge of the dish. A wide yellow ribbon may be tied round the cake to make it look more festive.

# BANANA TEA LOAF

*Serves 8-10*

225 g (8 oz) self-raising flour
½ teaspoon salt
½ teaspoon mixed spice
100 g (4 oz) butter, cut into pieces
50 g (2 oz) mixed peel
50 g (2 oz) currants
50 g (2 oz) walnut halves, chopped
450 g (1 lb) bananas, peeled
1 tablespoon clear honey
2 eggs, beaten
softened butter, to serve

*Preparation time: 20 minutes*
*Cooking time: 1¼ hours*
*Oven: 180°C, 350°F, Gas Mark 4*

1. Lightly grease a 1 kg (2 lb) loaf tin and set aside.
2. Sift the flour, salt and spice into a mixing bowl and

rub in the butter until the mixture resembles fine breadcrumbs.

3. Stir in the mixed peel, currants and walnuts.
4. Mash the bananas with the honey, and stir gently into the mixture with the beaten eggs. Blend well.
5. Pour the mixture into the prepared tin, and bake in a preheated oven for 1¼ hours, or until the loaf is well risen. Remove from the oven and allow to cool in the tin for 10 minutes. Turn on to a wire tray to cool.
6. Serve sliced and buttered. This loaf actually improves with keeping. It may be made up to 1 week in advance, then wrapped in cling film and stored in a cool place or be kept in an airtight container.

# RHUBARB AND GINGER JAM

*Makes 2.25 kg (5 lb) jam*

1.5 kg (3 lb) rhubarb, cut into chunks
1.5 kg (3 lb) preserving sugar
juice of 3 lemons
25 g (1 oz) ginger root, bruised and tied in muslin

*Preparation time: 30 minutes, plus overnight soaking*
*Cooking time: 1½ hours*

1. Take a large basin, and make layers with the rhubarb and sugar. Add the lemon juice and allow to stand overnight.
2. Next day, place the rhubarb mixture in a preserving pan, and add the ginger root. (It is best to tie the muslin bag loosely to one of the handles of the pan to make it easier to remove.)
3. Bring the mixture gently to the boil, then raise the heat and boil the jam rapidly until the temperature reaches 104°C, 220°F on the sugar thermometer. (If you do not possess a thermometer, you can test the setting point of the jam by spooning a little of the mixture on to a cold saucer and allowing it to cool. If the setting point has been reached, the surface will quickly set and will wrinkle up when pressed with the forefinger.) Remove the pan from the heat and allow to cool.
4. Remove the ginger root, spoon the jam into warm sterilized jam jars; cover and seal when cold.
5. Store in a cool place. The jam will keep for up to 6 months if kept cool and properly sealed.

*Simnel cake; Banana tea loaf; Rhubarb and ginger jam*

# BROWN SODA BREAD

One of the most traditional Irish breads.

225 g (8 oz) wholemeal flour
225 g (8 oz) plain white flour
1 teaspoon baking soda
3 teaspoons baking powder
2 teaspoons salt
450 ml (¾ pint) buttermilk or sour milk or 300 ml
(½ pint) natural unsweetened yoghurt and 150 ml
(¼ pint) water, mixed
warm milk or beaten egg, to glaze (optional)

*Preparation time: 15 minutes*
*Cooking time: 45-50 minutes*
*Oven: 190°C, 375°F, Gas Mark 5*

FROM THE TOP: *Barm brack; Irish whiskey cake; Spice bread; Brown soda bread* illustrated on page 104

1. Sift together the flours, baking soda, baking powder and salt. Tip in any bran left in the sieve.
2. Mix the buttermilk and beaten egg and stir in.
3. Knead on a floured surface for a few minutes until smooth, then shape by hand either into a round flat cake, or put into a 1 kg (2 lb) greased loaf tin.
4. Make a deep cross on the round or cut down the middle of the tin to ensure even distribution in rising, and bake in a preheated oven for 40-45 minutes.
5. If a glaze is required, take out and brush with a little warm milk or beaten egg and put back in the oven for about 5 minutes.
6. Wrap in a tea towel to keep the crust soft and cool before cutting. [F]
7. If preferred the mixture can be shaped into small scones and baked for 15 minutes.

[F] When completely cold these loaves will freeze very well sealed in a plastic bag. Thaw out for at least 3 hours before cutting.

# SPICE BREAD

*Makes one 1 kg (2 lb) loaf*

275 g (10 oz) self-raising flour, sifted
1 teaspoon mixed spice
½ teaspoon ground ginger
100 g (4 oz) light brown sugar
25 g (1 oz) candied peel, chopped
175 g (6 oz) sultanas
50 g (2 oz) butter
100 g (4 oz) golden syrup
1 egg (size l), beaten
4 tablespoons milk

*Preparation time: 30 minutes*
*Cooking time: 1¼ hours*
*Oven: 180°C, 350°F, Gas Mark 4;*
*then: 160°C, 325°F, Gas Mark 3*

1. Sift the flour with the spice and ginger, then add the brown sugar, candied peel and sultanas. Make a well in the centre.
2. Melt the butter with the golden syrup over a low heat, but do not allow it to become too hot.
3. Pour into the well and mix thoroughly.
4. Mix the beaten egg with the milk and add to the flour, mixing very well.
5. Pour the mixture into a greased 1 kg (2 lb) loaf tin, levelling off the top.
6. Bake in a preheated oven for 30 minutes, then lower the heat and cook for another 45 minutes. Test with a thin skewer before taking out. The skewer should come out clean if the loaf is cooked.
7. Turn out on to a wire tray to cool.

# BARM BRACK

*Makes 3 cakes*

450 g (1 lb) sultanas
450 g (1 lb) raisins
450 g (1 lb) brown sugar
3 cups of milkless tea
450 g (1 lb) plain flour
3 eggs, beaten
3 teaspoons baking powder
3 teaspoons mixed spice
1 tablespoon honey, warmed

*Preparation time: 30 minutes, plus overnight soaking*
*Cooking time: 1½ hours*
*Oven: 160°C, 325°F, Gas Mark 3*

1. Soak the fruit and sugar in the tea overnight.
2. The next day add the rest of the ingredients except the honey and mix very well.
3. Lightly grease three 20 cm (8 inch) round tins and divide the mixture between them, levelling off the tops.
4. Bake in a preheated oven for 1½ hours, then take out and brush the tops with a little warmed honey to glaze.
5. Put back in the oven for 5 minutes to dry.
6. Cool on a wire tray.

# IRISH WHISKEY CAKE

*Makes 1 × 17.5 cm (7 inch) cake*

peel of 1 large lemon
85 ml (3 fl oz) Irish whiskey
175 g (6 oz) butter
175 g (6 oz) caster sugar
3 eggs, separated
175 g (6 oz) plain flour, sifted
175 g (6 oz) sultanas
pinch of salt
1 teaspoon baking powder

*Preparation time: 30 minutes, plus overnight soaking*
*Cooking time: 1½-1¾ hours*
*Oven: 180°C, 350°F, Gas Mark 4*

1. Put the lemon peel into a glass, cover with the whiskey and leave overnight, covered.
2. Cream the butter and sugar until light. Add the egg yolks one at a time with a spoonful of sifted flour, mixing well.
3. Strain the whiskey into it and add the sultanas with 2 tablespoons flour.
4. Whisk the egg whites stiffly and fold into the mixture with the remaining flour mixed with the salt and baking powder. See that the mixture is well amalgamated.
5. Pour into a greased and lined 17.5 cm (7 inch) cake tin and bake in a preheated oven for 1½-1¾ hours. Test with a skewer before taking from the oven – the skewer should come out clean.
6. Cool for 5 minutes in the tin, then turn out on to a wire tray and remove the paper.

# INDEX

**Acknowledgements**

Illustrations by Magda Lazou.
Recipe selection and introduction by Rosemary Wilkinson.
For the photography on the cover and pages 2–3, 8–9, 28–29, 44–45, 62–63,
84–85, 104–105, the publishers would like to thank the following:
Photographer: Sue Atkinson
Photographic stylist: Janet Rhind-Cutt
Food prepared for photography: Sandra Baddeley

All other photography from the Octopus Group Picture Library:

Laurie Evans: pages 11, 12, 13, 14, 15, 30, 31, 32, 33, 34, 35, 36, 37, 38, 42, 43,
46, 47, 48, 50, 56, 57, 58, 59, 61, 65, 75, 78, 79, 86, 87, 97, 98, 99, 101, 106, 110,
111, 113, 114, 115, 117, 124, 125

James Jackson: pages 16, 17, 18, 19, 25, 26, 27, 66, 67, 69, 92, 93, 108, 109, 118,
119, 120, 121

Vernon Morgan: pages 21, 22, 41, 53, 55, 70, 73, 76, 80, 82, 83, 88, 90,
91, 95, 102, 103

The publishers would also like to thank the following for lending equipment used
in the photography of this book:

Dee's Antiques, 34 Frances Road, Windsor, Berks

Turk's Head Antiques, 98 High Street, Eton, Berks

Wargrave Antiques, 5 High Street, Wargrave, Berks